COCKTAILS & MIXED DRINKS

COCKTAILS &

Lansdowne

Sydney Auckland London New York

MIXED DRINKS

EDDIE TIRADO
PHOTOGRAPHY BY RAY JOYCE

Contents

INTRODUCTION

The origin of the cocktail is obscure but we do know that it was first
made popular in America and from there, as drinking habits grew more
sophisticated, its popularity spread throughout the world.
The number of cocktail recipes available is virtually limitless and a
creative bartender can find endless inspiration for really original drinks
at any time. This book aims to simplify cocktail mixing for those who
like to entertain at home and to teach the basics of mixing cocktails
so that the enthusiast will then want to experiment and
even devise new cocktails.

What is a Cocktail?

'Vive le cocktail' toasted a Frenchman in Betsy's Tavern near Yorktown during the American Revolution after seeing bottles decorated with cocks' tails. He was probably thinking more about the chicken he was eating than the drink but this is the American version of how the name 'cocktail' originated. Another definition of the word cocktail refers to the special way of cutting a horse's tail. However, the connection between a horse's tail and drinking a rather delicate blend of spirit, liquor and fruit juice has us baffled.

The word 'cocktail', when put in front of the word 'bar' in any of our hotels or eateries, should cultivate thoughts of pleasant surroundings, quiet background music, (sometimes even a pianist) and subdued lighting, and behind the bar the cocktail barman (or bartender). This man (and it is frequently a woman) who provides not only good spirits, but a ready smile, a friendly word, a sympathetic ear and even a shoulder to cry upon, also has that little extra knowledge about drinks and their mixing than anyone else. He takes his task of mixing your drink most seriously as he realises that he has a standard to maintain.

A cocktail is in fact a drink consisting of two or more ingredients, stirred or shaken, as a short or long drink as required. It has been said that the first cocktail was a martini but this cannot be proved, but we can take it with an olive or a twist of lemon – not a pinch of salt!

For the 'mixologist', or the host at home mixing his own concoction, there are two set rules: All clear drinks, i.e. those not containing fruit juice, cream or milk, must be stirred with ice, e.g. Martinis and Manhattans.
Those drinks containing fruit juices and cream, etc. must be shaken either by hand or with an electric blender to acquire a perfect blend, e.g. Brandy Alexander.

Further Tips for Successful Drink Mixing

If possible pour your cocktails into chilled glasses for a warm cocktail is undrinkable. Chill the glasses either in the refrigerator or by putting three cubes of ice in the glass while you are mixing the drink and then discarding these ice cubes just before serving the drink. Equipment for chilling glasses is also available in retail stores.

Almost all drinks taste better when served ice cold; therefore have plenty of clear, clean ice on hand when you entertain. The ice should be shaved, cracked or in cubes. Ice should always be placed in the mixing glass, shaker or glass before liquor is added for this chills the drink quickly and thoroughly.

If only cubed ice is available place the ice in a tea towel and hit it with a mallet on a hard surface to obtain cracked ice. Do *not* use a glass bottle for crushing ice.

Wherever possible use fresh lemon or orange juice in a drink. However, concentrated juice is almost as good. Keep slices of orange, lemon or lime fresh, by covering with a damp cloth and placing them in the refrigerator.

When cutting lemon, orange or lime peel, never include the white membrane of the rind. Shave off only the coloured surface peel in strips about 13 to 20 millimetres (½ to ¾ inches) wide.

Don't fill the shaker so full that there is no room for shaking. Use a short, sharp shaking action (do not rock) when mixing cocktails.

Cocktails should be drunk as soon as possible after serving.

Be sure that your glasses are clean and polished and have no chips or cracks.

Always handle glasses by the stem or base.

Cherry or peel is always added to the cocktail after it has been shaken or mixed.

Where a twist of orange or lemon peel is stated, the oil of the peel should be squeezed on top of the cocktail and the peel then dropped in the drink, unless otherwise requested.
Always bear in mind that bad mixing and bad presentation will ruin any cocktail or mixed drink no matter how good the recipe or the ingredients.

Setting up Your Own Bar

One of the most important assets the home entertainer can have is a bar and the necessary equipment for mixing and serving drinks. This bar can vary from the elaborate to the very simple; from a complete room set aside as a bar area in a house to a table or traymobile being used for this purpose beside a swimming pool or on the patio. If you have the time, patience and skill, you can make your own bar, if not then you can purchase a bar from any of the large department or furniture stores.

There are many types of bars but they mainly fall into three categories – mobile or portable, semi-permanent and permanent.

The mobile bar

This bar can be moved from place to place which enables you to entertain in such areas as the patio, barbecue and swimming pool at the same time; for it allows you to move, as a whole unit, your equipment, glasses and spirits, etc. to the area from which you wish to serve. The main drawback to this type of bar is the lack of washing facilities for glasses.

There are many variations of the mobile bar and a popular one is the small imitation keg which opens out showing the provision for glasses and a few bottles within.

The semi-permanent bar

This type of bar tends to be a feature of the room, e.g. a cocktail cabinet, whereas a portable bar is easily hidden from view. An advantage of the semi-permanent bar is that you are able to attractively and conveniently display your equipment and glasses and even the range of spirits you have available. But keep in mind when positioning this bar that it must be as close as practicable to washing facilities.

The permanent bar

This bar forms an integral part of the interior decoration and design of a room. It can be set up so that everything is readily accessible to the person serving drinks. In this bar, if finance is available, you can really let your head go by installing a sink with hot and cold water, refrigerator and all number of 'non-essential' bar luxuries. And on this bar your equipment and spirits can be displayed at best advantage. To be really eye-catching and effective this bar must be a showpiece in the room. Ideally the front of the bar should be illuminated by indirect lighting as should the area behind the bar. Lighting plays a most important part in the usefulness and appearance of the bar but it should be subdued. As well, the lighting, if used properly, will enhance the interior of the room in which the bar is situated.

Shelving

Shelves of glass on the wall behind the bar look attractive. To support the shelves, use metal strips with brackets which fit at various intervals into these strips. These can be purchased in various colours from most hardware stores. This type of shelving can be adjusted for displaying glasses or bottles, and it provides an ideal place for showing off fine glassware, spirits and other items.

If you decide to build your own bar, bear in mind that the height of the bar should be comfortable for a person to sit at with his drink resting on the top of the bar. Between 1 metre and 1.2 metres (3 feet and 3 feet 6 inches) is best and enables you to use an ordinary kitchen stool as a bar stool. Bar stools can be expensive but a handyman with a flair for upholstery can take a piece of foam covered with vinyl and transform a kitchen stool into an attractive bar stool.

Bar Equipment

The following basic equipment should be acquired: cocktail shaker (most popular is the 'Boston'; or 'American' or 'Standard'), or if you have a blender better still; mixing glass and spoon; spirit measures 15 ml and 30 ml (½ and 1 ounce); ice bucket and tongs; 'Hawthorn' strainer; corkscrew; can opener; bottle opener; fruit squeezer; fruit knife and board which can double as a cheese board; swizzle sticks; toothpicks; coasters; serviettes; soda syphon; salt and pepper; nutmeg; cinnamon; a cloth for drying glasses; bottle stoppers for recorking carbonated drinks; oranges; lemons; maraschino cherries; olives and cocktail onions; straws.

Basic Bottle Stock Required to Serve Standard Cocktails

Scotch whisky
Australian whisky
Bourbon whiskey
Rye whisky
Brandy (many excellent
Australian brands)
Cognac
Gin
Vodka
Tequila
White rum
Dark rum
Dry and sweet vermouth
Grenadine
Angostura bitters and orange bitters

Liqueurs (cordials)

Advokaat
Cherry brandy
Crème de Cacao
Crème de menthe
Cointreau
Drambuie
Galliano
Grand Marnier
Tia Maria

There are many other liqueurs available so check the glossary (page 108) for taste preferences and then buy accordingly.

Mixers

Soda water
Dry ginger ale
Cola
Lemonade or 7-up
Bitter lemon
Tonic water
Mineral water
Orange juice
Lemon juice
Lime juice
Pineapple juice
Tomato juice

Glasses for the Bar

Glass is a hard, brittle and usually transparent substance made by fusing silica, an alkali, and a base. Legend ascribes its invention to the Phoenicians and the general manufacturing process has varied little from the days of ancient Egypt to modern Europe. The champagne glass (as we know it in Australia) has an interesting history. In the eighteenth century King Louis XVI considered Marie Antoinette such a creature of beauty that a glass should be designed to cover her breast and thus the champagne glass was born. A further stipulation was that only the wine of France was to be drunk from this shaped glass. This type of champagne glass is no longer used in Europe because its width allows the gas to escape causing the champagne to go flat in a short time. The tulip-type glass is popularly used by champagne drinkers today, for its length helps retain gas in champagne for a much longer period.

Glassware is more flexible for the home entertainer than it is for the professional bartender. For example, a tulip glass can be used as a sour glass or a highball glass can be used as a Zombie glass. A well equipped bar needs the following types of glasses: a shot glass (used for straight spirit without ice; it is most commonly used in the United States for 'Boilermakers'); a 30 ml (1 fl oz) liqueur glass; a 90-120 ml (3-4 fl oz) sherry glass; a 150 ml (5 fl oz) stemmed wine glass; a 210 ml (7 fl oz) stemmed wine glass; a whisky glass (sizes vary); a cocktail glass (these are usually 90 ml or 3 fl oz); a 180 ml (6 fl oz) old-fashioned glass; a 180 ml (6 fl oz) champagne glass; a 300 ml (10 fl oz) highball glass; beer glass (see page 107, as sizes vary) and a brandy balloon or snifter.

Whether your glassware is costly crystal or less expensive ware from the supermarket take great care of it. Wash each glass separately in reasonably hot water, rinse, and then dry with a clean, lint-free glass-cloth while the glass is still warm from the water. Glasses should be aired before they are returned to their shelves. Handle glasses by the stem or base so they retain their high polish for later use.

Giving a Party and Enjoying It

Hospitality has two essential components: a sincere and congenial host and good preparation. Always keep your kitchen cupboard well-stocked in case of unexpected guests and make sure your bar contains a fair supply of drinks.

Once you have organized your main supplies of food and refreshments take a mental check (or even have a prepared list) to make sure you have everything you are likely to need. In the bar you should have two glasses per guest, serving trays, water jugs, soda syphon, bar tools, knife and board for cutting on, fruit juice, fresh cream, oranges, lemons, cucumber, pickled onions, maraschino cherries, mint, toothpicks, glass-cloths, a sponge for mopping up, and an abundance of party ice.

Guide to liquor requirements

There is no way to calculate exactly but working on the assumption that you serve 30 ml (1 oz) of spirit per drink, a 750 ml (26 fl oz) bottle will produce 26 drinks. Aperitifs are an exception and call for 60 to 90 ml (2 to 3 fl oz) per drink. The average cocktail glass contains 90 ml (3 fl oz) of liquid which comprise spirit or liqueur (cordial) and the basic ingredients of fruit juices or cream. Your needs will vary depending on the size of the drinks (if you value your carpet never fill the glass to the top) and the mood of your guests. It is wise to be overstocked as one very well-known toast implies: 'One bottle for the four of us! Thank God there are no more of us!' Always allow 2 glasses per person for each type of drink served.

Basic drink stock

The following is a guide to basic stock required, but if you know your guests' preferences, this can be adjusted.

Scotch and/or a blended whisky; vodka; gin; rum; brandy; dry and sweet vermouth; sherry or Dubonnet; red and white wine (economically obtained in flagons or casks), liqueurs and of course beer.

Soft drinks should include soda water, dry ginger, tonic water, bitter lemon, lemonade, your favourite cola, orange and lemon squash, mineral water and do not forget a bottle of bitters.

Juices, either fresh or frozen should include tomato, orange, lemon, pineapple, and lime.

Garnishes to have on hand are lemons, oranges, cherries and olives.

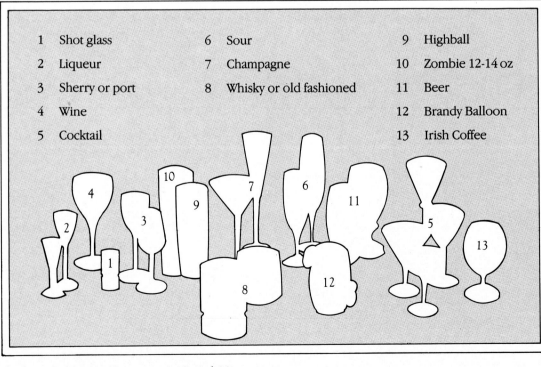

1	Shot glass	6	Sour	9	Highball
2	Liqueur	7	Champagne	10	Zombie 12-14 oz
3	Sherry or port	8	Whisky or old fashioned	11	Beer
4	Wine			12	Brandy Balloon
5	Cocktail			13	Irish Coffee

Outline of photograph on pages 10 and 11.

Helpful hints for the bartender-host

Carbonated beverages should be the last ingredient added to a drink.

A good tip if you are planning drinks containing sugar – make up in advance a sugar syrup containing 1 cup of sugar added to 1 cup of water. Bring to the boil and simmer until sugar is dissolved. This can be bottled and refrigerated and will keep indefinitely. It cuts down the barman's job of trying to dissolve sugar in drinks.

As with food or snacks, prepare the bar in advance. Fruit juices should be squeezed and oranges and lemon which are required for garnishing should be sliced fairly thick, about 6 mm (¼ inch) as they do not curl or drop. When cutting peel for a twist, take only the coloured rind, not the pulp as it is bitter. Pre-cut fruit into slices and twists and they will keep fresh if covered by a damp cloth or plastic wrap and refrigerated.

If the washing machine is handy to the kitchen, it can be good place to store ice as it keeps cold and avoids the mess caused when it melts.

Do not forget the teetotallers at the party, and have a choice of non-alcoholic drinks available for them.

So with good preparation beforehand, congenial company, well-mixed drinks and attractively presented dishes you will be a relaxed host and your party will be well on its way to success.

Measures

Measurements for all drink recipes are given in metric, with their imperial equivalent in parentheses. A dash is equal to 1/6 of a teaspoon (or the equivalent to a flick of the wrist) but add the amount to suit individual tastes; 1 teaspoon = 5 ml (1/6 fl oz); 1 tablespoon = 18 ml (3/5 fl oz); 1 jigger = 30 ml (1 fl oz); 1 gill = 150 ml (5 fl oz or ¼ pint); 1 pint = 600 ml (20 fl oz) = 10 to 12 servings. Unless stated otherwise the quantity in each recipe is for one drink.

The standard 750 ml bottle has a slightly greater capacity than its imperial equivalent of 26 fl oz. The imperial equivalent of a 375 ml bottle is 13 fl oz; and the imperial equivalent of a 1.5 litre bottle is 40 fl oz.

For bar sales, the half-nip measures 15 ml (½ fl oz); the nip measures 30 ml (1 fl oz).

The Silver Fox, Eddie Tirado – always the perfect host.

Whisky

Whisky is a spirit obtained from distillation of a fermented mash (prepared ingredients before fermentation) of grain (barley, maize and rice mainly) and aged in wood.
There are approximately 200 brands of whiskies available in Australia and these can be divided into seven types: Scotch, Irish, Canadian, Bourbon, Tennessee Whiskey, American Blended, Australian.

SCOTCH WHISKY

Scotch whisky is a distinctive product of Scotland where it is believed that the first whisky was born in the Highlands in the sixteenth century. Its Gaelic name 'Usquebaugh' meaning 'water of life' was later anglicised to 'whisky'. Two types of whiskies are necessary to produce Scotch – Scotch malt whisky which gives the blend body and character, and Scotch grain whisky which is used for lightness.

In the production of Scotch two distillation processes are used: (a) the pot-still process (b) the patent or coffey-still process.

Scotch malt whisky is made from malted barley only and is manufactured by the pot-still process:

Cleaning – the barley is cleaned to remove any foreign matter.

Malting – the selected barley is steeped in water for two or three days. It is then spread on a concrete floor to germinate for eight to twelve days while the starch in the barley kernels is converted into sugar.

Drying and grinding – growth is stopped at a certain time and the barley is subjected to heat over fires of smokeless coal and peat; the peat imparts its flavour and aroma during this process. The dried malt is then ground.

Mashing – the ground barley is crushed with hot water and the conversion of soluble starch into maltose is completed. The liquid produced (wort) is drawn off and the remaining husks removed for cattle food.

Fermentation – the wort is cooled and then passed into vessels called washbacks where it is fermented by yeast which attacks the sugar and converts it into crude alcohol, known as 'wash'.

Distillation – malt whisky is distilled twice in potstills. The 'wash' is heated, and as alcohol has a lower boiling point than water, it becomes vapour which is then cooled and condensed back into liquid.

Maturation – this new whisky is poured into oak wood casks where it is matured into a pleasant mellow spirit for as long as fifteen years.

Scotch grain whisky is made from unmalted barley with a mixture of maize, and distilled by the patent-still process which differs from the pot-still process in four ways:

The mash consists of a proportion of malt and unmalted cereals.

The grain and water are agitated by stirrers during steam pressure cooking to burst the starch cells in the grain and to convert starch into maltose.

The liquid (worts) is collected at specific gravity lower than that produced in the pot-still process.

Distillation by this still is a continous process and the spirit is collected at a much higher strength and does not require as long to mature as malt whisky distilled in the pot-still.

After the malt whiskies and grain whiskies are matured, they are blended or 'married' to achieve consistent quality and bouquet. There may be as many as forty different malt and grain whiskies blended according to a secret formula handed down from generation to generation, to produce the Scotch Whisky we know today.

Some very popular Scotch-based drinks are: 30 ml (1 fl oz) Scotch over ice topped up with soda water, Scotch with dry ginger ale, Scotch with coke and Scotch with mineral water. For variation try a lemon peel in your Scotch.

SCOTCH MIST

ice
60 ml (2 fl oz) Scotch
twist of lemon peel

Pour the Scotch into a shaker with ice.
Add a twist of lemon peel.
Shake and pour into an old-fashioned glass.

GODFATHER

23 ml (¾ fl oz) Amaretto di Galliano
45 ml (1½ fl oz) Scotch Whisky
ice
maraschino cherry
slice of orange

Serve in an old-fashioned glass with ice. Garnish with a cherry and a slice of orange.

BLUE BLAZER

60 ml (2 fl oz) Scotch
60 ml (2 fl oz) boiling water
sugar
lemon peel
2 mugs

Using (preferably) two silver or copper mugs; pour whisky into one mug and boiling water into the other.
Ignite the whisky and while burning mix both ingredients by pouring five times from one mug to the other.
Sugar to taste.
Decorate with lemon peel and serve.

IRISH WHISKEY

BOILERMAKER

Serve 1 large jigger of Scotch straight, with a glass of beer as a chaser.

KILT

60 ml (2 fl oz) Scotch whisky
1/2 banana
150 ml (5 fl oz) milk
ice
2 maraschino cherries

Put the whisky, banana and milk into a blender with ice, strain and serve in a highball glass, garnished with cherries.

GOLDEN OLDIE

30 ml (1 fl oz) Scotch whisky
30 ml (1 fl oz) Galliano
30 ml (1 fl oz) orange juice
ice
maraschino cherry
slice of orange

Serve in an old-fashioned glass with ice. Garnish with a cherry and slice of orange.

WHISKY ON THE ROCKS

Serve 60 ml (2 fl oz) Scotch in an old-fashioned glass with ice.

Irish Whiskey is made from a mash of cereal grains, mostly barley, with perhaps 20 percent oats and wheat, in a manner similar to the malts of Scotland. It is distilled in pot-stills. (A pot-still is an old-fashioned, fat-bellied, tapered neck still requiring two distinct operations to produce a useful spirit. It is used exclusively for straight whiskies.) Triple distillation and long maturation contribute to the uniqueness of Irish Whiskey for even the youngest is aged in sherry casks for at least seven years. Irish Whiskeys were mostly straight whiskeys but now a number of blended (malt and grain) are available and are found to be a lighter-boiled product.
The Irish have many toasts to compliment their whiskey and the following is just one:

'Health and long life to you
Land without rent to you
The woman of your choice to you
More land every year to you
And rest in Erin.'

COOL WATERS

45 ml (1 1/2 fl oz) Irish whiskey
30 ml (1 fl oz) Midori liqueur
ice
water
1/4 slice lime

Pour Irish whiskey and Midori liqueur into a highball glass with ice. Top up with water and add 1/4 slice of a lime.

IRISH ON THE ROCKS

Pour 45 ml (1 1/2 fl oz) Irish whiskey into a glass of ice and serve.

FLYING IRISHMAN

60 ml (2 fl oz) Irish whiskey
30 ml (1 fl oz) Cinzano sweet vermouth
ice
green cherry

Stir in a mixing glass with ice. Strain into a cocktail glass and garnish with a green cherry.

MORNING GLORY

45 ml (1 1/2 fl oz) Scotch
white of one egg
1 teaspoon caster (powdered) sugar
ice
soda water

Shake Scotch, egg white and sugar, then strain into a highball glass with ice.
Top with soda water and serve.

WHISKY COBBLER

cracked ice
60 ml (2 fl oz) Scotch
4 dashes curaçao
4 dashes brandy
slice of lemon
fruit for garnish
sprig of mint

Fill a goblet with cracked ice.
Add the Scotch, curaçao, brandy and a slice of lemon. Stir, decorate with fruit and a sprig of mint, and serve.

ROB ROY

1/2 Scotch
1/2 sweet vermouth
dash Angostura bitters
ice
maraschino cherry

Stir the Scotch, vermouth and bitters in a mixing glass with ice.
Pour into a cocktail glass.
Add a cherry and serve.

MAMIE TAYLOR

60 ml (2 fl oz) Scotch
ice
ginger ale
slice of lemon

Serve the Scotch in a 300 ml (10 fl oz) glass with ice. Top with ginger ale and a slice of lemon.

BOBBY BURNS

1/2 Scotch
1/4 dry vermouth
1/4 sweet vermouth
1 dash Benedictine
ice cubes
lemon peel

Stir Scotch, dry and sweet vermouth and Benedictine with ice and serve in a cocktail glass. Garnish with a twist of lemon peel.

WHISKY MILK PUNCH

60 ml (2 fl oz) Scotch
300 ml (10 fl oz) milk
1 1/2 teaspoons sugar
ice
nutmeg

Shake Scotch, milk and sugar with ice and strain into a highball glass. Sprinkle nutmeg on top and serve.

IRISH EYES

Created by Eddie Tirado

45 ml (1½ fl oz) Irish whiskey
60 ml (2 fl oz) green crème de menthe
60 ml (2 fl oz) fresh cream
ice
2 green cherries

Shake whiskey, crème de menthe and fresh cream with ice and strain into a champagne glass. Garnish with a cherry on a toothpick and serve.

IRISH COFFEE

hot black coffee
sugar
45 ml (1½ fl oz) Irish whiskey
lightly-whipped fresh cream

Fill a 240 ml (8 fl oz) glass with hot black coffee and add sugar to taste. Add Irish whiskey. Float cream on top but do not stir. Serve.

LEPRECHAUN DANCER

Created by Eddie Tirado

60 ml (2 fl oz) Irish whiskey
15 ml (½ fl oz) lemon juice
soda water
dry ginger ale
twist of lemon peel

Serve whiskey and lemon juice with ice in a highball glass. Top with soda water and dry ginger ale in equal parts. Put a twist of lemon peel in the glass.

MANHATTAN (DRY)

45 ml (1¹/₂ fl oz) Canadian whisky
23 ml (³/₄ fl oz) dry vermouth
1 or 2 dashes Angostura bitters (optional)
ice
twist of lemon or 1 olive

Stir whisky, vermouth and bitters with ice and strain into a cocktail glass. Add a twist of lemon or olive and serve.

DESHLER COCKTAIL

23 ml (³/₄ fl oz) Canadian whisky
23 ml (³/₄ fl oz) Dubonnet
2 dashes Cointreau
2 dashes bitters
cracked ice
lemon peel
orange peel

Shake whisky, Dubonnet, Cointreau and bitters with cracked ice. Strain into a chilled cocktail glass. Twist lemon and orange peel over the drink and serve.

BLINKER COCKTAIL

15 ml (¹/₂ fl oz) Canadian whisky
23 ml (³/₄ fl oz) grapefruit juice
8 ml (¹/₄ fl oz) grenadine
cracked ice

Shake whisky, grapefruit juice and grenadine with cracked ice. Serve in a chilled cocktail glass.

CANADIAN WHISKY

The principal grains used in Canadian Whisky are corn, rye and barley malt. The proportion of grain used, and the distilling and re-distilling processes are the trade secrets of the master distiller. Canadian Whisky is a product of blended whiskies which may be blended before ageing or during the ageing period. Maturation takes place in charred white oak barrels for two or more years but most Canadian Whiskies are at least six years of age.

EDWARD VIII COCKTAIL

45 ml (1 1/2 fl oz) Canadian whisky
1 dash Pernod
2 teaspoons Italian vermouth
2 teaspoons water
1 piece orange peel
ice

Stir whisky, Pernod, vermouth, water and orange peel with ice in an old-fashioned glass and serve.

NEW YORK COCKTAIL

60 ml (2 fl oz) Canadian whisky
juice of 1/2 lemon
4 dashes grenadine
ice
orange peel

Shake whisky, lemon juice and grenadine with ice. Strain into a cocktail glass. Garnish with a twist of orange peel and serve.

WARD EIGHT NO 1

45 ml (1 1/2 fl oz) Canadian whisky
30 ml (1 fl oz) lemon juice
8 ml (1/4 fl oz) grenadine
1/2 teaspoon caster (powdered) sugar
cracked ice
fruit for garnish

Shake whisky, lemon juice, grenadine and sugar with cracked ice.
Strain into a cocktail glass.
Garnish with fruit.
Serve with drinking straws.

WARD EIGHT NO 2

45 ml (1 1/2 fl oz) rye whisky
15 ml (1/2 fl oz) orange juice
15 ml (1/2 fl oz) lemon juice
1 teaspoon grenadine
cracked ice

Shake whisky, orange and lemon juice, and grenadine with cracked ice.
Strain into a cocktail glass and serve.

CARLTON COCKTAIL

30 ml (1 fl oz) Canadian whisky
15 ml (1/2 fl oz) orange juice
15 ml (1/2 fl oz) Cointreau
cracked ice

Shake whisky, orange juice and Cointreau with cracked ice. Strain into a chilled cocktail glass and serve.

OLD-FASHIONED COCKTAIL

1 dash bitters
1 cube of sugar
ice
2 dashes soda or water
60 ml (2 fl oz) Canadian whisky
1/2 slice of orange
1 maraschino cherry
twist of lemon

Use an old-fashioned glass. In it put a cube of sugar covered with a dash of bitters.
Add soda water or water.
Muddle this, then add ice.
Add whisky.
Place 1/2 slice of orange and a cherry on a toothpick on the side of the glass.
Put a twist of lemon in the glass and serve with a swizzle stick.
Note: The most popular spirit used is rye or bourbon, but any base can be used.

Some very popular drinks made with Canadian whisky are:
Canadian whisky over ice topped with soda water, Canadian whisky with cola, Canadian whisky with mineral water, Canadian whisky with lemonade, and Canadian whisky with 3 parts lemonade and 1 part dry ginger ale, with a twist of lemon.

BOURBON

The Rev. Elijah Craig is credited with production of the first Bourbon Whiskey in 1789 in Bourbon County in the United States; but it was not until May 1964, that a resolution was passed by the U.S. Senate and the House of Representatives recognising bourbon as a 'distinctive product of the United States'. Most bourbons are straight whiskeys which means that they are obtained from a spirit distilled from grain (not less than 51 percent corn) and aged in new charred oak barrels for at least two years.
Sour mash whiskey is made through a variation of the fermentation method. The distiller uses part of a previous day's mash, instead of fresh mash and fresh yeast as in the fermentation of bourbon, thus each batch is 'related' to the previous batch.

PINK PANTHER

30 ml (1 fl oz) bourbon
15 ml (1/2 fl oz) vodka
30 ml (1 fl oz) coconut milk
dash grenadine
30 ml (1 fl oz) cream

Shake ingredients with ice and serve in a champagne glass.

BOURBON ON THE ROCKS

Pour 45 ml (1½ fl oz) bourbon over ice in an old-fashioned glass.

Some very popular bourbon drinks are: 30 ml (1 fl oz) bourbon over ice topped with soda, bourbon with cola, bourbon with dry ginger ale, bourbon with lemonade and bourbon with mineral water.

BOURBON MANHATTAN

2/3 bourbon
1/3 sweet vermouth
dash of Angostura bitters
maraschino cherry
ice

Stir bourbon, vermouth, bitters and ice and pour into a cocktail glass and garnish with cherry.

TOOTSIE

30 ml (1 fl oz) Jim Beam bourbon
15 ml (1/2 fl oz) Galliano
dash grenadine
orange juice
ice

Top bourbon, Galliano and grenadine with orange juice and shake together with ice. Serve in a highball glass.

TENNESSEE WHISKEY

The production of Tennessee Whiskey begins with the sour mash process similar to the method described for bourbon, but is definitely not bourbon. It differs in the extra steps that take place immediately after distillation when the whiskey is seeped slowly, very slowly, through vats packed with charcoal. The charcoal comes from the sugar maple tree which grows in the wooded parts of the Tennessee Highlands. It is this charcoal which contributes so much to the character of Tennessee whiskey.
Tennessee whiskey may be served with: tonic water, soda water, mineral water, dry ginger ale, cola, 7-up or lemonade or orange juice.

TENNESSEE SNIFTER

Warm a brandy balloon by pouring warm water over it.
Dry the glass. Add 90 ml (3 fl oz) Tennessee whiskey. Sip and enjoy the drink.

SWEET MARIA

30 ml (1 fl oz) Tia Maria
30 ml (1 fl oz) bourbon
30 ml (1 fl oz) cream or 1 scoop of ice cream
1 strawberry
nutmeg

Shake or blend ingredients with ice and strain into a champagne glass.
Garnish with a strawberry and dust with nutmeg.

LENA COCKTAIL

(This was the winner of the International Cocktail Competition held in Tokyo in 1971.)

5/10 Old Grand-dad bourbon
2/10 Martini Rossi vermouth
1/10 dry vermouth
1/10 Campari
1/10 Galliano
1 maraschino cherry

Stir bourbon, Martini Rossi vermouth, dry vermouth, Campari and Galliano in a mixing glass. Serve with a cherry.

BOURBON MINT JULEP

60 ml (2 fl oz) bourbon
1/2 teaspoon sugar
4 sprigs mint
cracked ice
dash dark rum or brandy
mint, lemon and cherry for garnish

Muddle bourbon, sugar and mint.
Fill a highball glass with cracked ice.
Add ingredients and stir till the outside of the glass is frosted.
Top with a dash of dark rum or brandy.
Garnish with a sprig of mint, lemon and cherry. Serve with straws.

TENNESSEE MANHATTAN (DRY)

45 ml (1 1/2 fl oz) Tennessee whiskey
23 ml (3/4 fl oz) dry vermouth
1 or 2 dashes Angostura bitters
ice
twist of lemon or 1 olive

Stir whiskey, vermouth and bitters with ice and strain into a cocktail glass.
Add a twist of lemon or olive and serve.

TENNESSEE SOUR

juice of 1/2 lemon
1/2 teaspoon sugar
60 ml (2 fl oz) Tennessee whiskey
ice
soda water
1/2 slice orange and maraschino cherry

Shake the juice, sugar, whiskey and ice.
Strain into a sour glass.
Top up if desired with soda water.
Garnish with orange
and cherry.

ADAM AND EVE OLD-FASHIONED

Created by Eddie Tirado

1 lump sugar
dash bitters
soda water
3 cubes ice
60 ml (2 fl oz) Tennessee whiskey
15 ml (1/2 fl oz) Galliano

Place sugar and bitters in an old-fashioned glass.
Add enough soda water to cover the sugar.
Muddle well.
Add ice cubes.
Pour whiskey over this.
Float Galliano on top and serve.

WHISKEY COLLINS

60 ml (2 fl oz) blended whiskey
juice of 1/2 lemon
1 teaspoon caster (powdered) sugar
slice of lemon
slice of orange
cherry

Shake whiskey, lemon juice and sugar with ice and pour into a Collins glass. Fill with carbonated water and stir. Decorate with a slice of lemon, orange and a cherry. Serve with a straw.

WHISKEY RICKEY

45 ml (1 1/2 fl oz) blended whiskey
juice of 1/2 lime
soda water or club soda
slice of lime

Pour lime juice into a highball glass over ice, add whiskey and fill with soda water. Decorate with lime

WHISKEY DAISY

60 ml (2 fl oz) blended whiskey
1 teaspoon grenadine
juice of 1/2 lemon
1/2 teaspoon caster (powdered) sugar

Shake ingredients with ice and strain into a 180 ml (6 fl oz) goblet and garnish with fruit.

BESSIE AND JESSIE

60 ml (2 fl oz) American Blended whiskey
180 ml (6 fl oz) milk
ice
30 ml (1 fl oz) advokaat

Shake whiskey and milk with ice and pour into a highball glass.
Float the advokaat on top and serve.

WHISKEY TODDY (HOT)

Put a lump of sugar into a whiskey glass and fill two-thirds with hot water. Add 60 ml (2 fl oz) blended whiskey. Stir and garnish with a slice of lemon then sprinkle nutmeg on top.
It can be served cold by using cold water.

GRINGO COCKTAIL

45 ml (1½ fl oz) blended whiskey
30 ml (1 fl oz) coconut milk
60 ml (2 fl oz) pineapple juice
30 ml (1 fl oz) cream
15 ml (½ fl oz) banana liqueur
slice of pineapple
strawberry
sprig of mint

Shake ingredients and pour over ice in a highball glass. Garnish with a slice of pineapple, a strawberry and sprig of mint. A green cherry and a red cherry may also be added for further garnish.

BLENDED WHISKEY

These whiskeys usually contain at least 20 percent (by volume or 100 proof) straight whiskey, separately or in combination with other whiskey or neutral spirits, and is bottled at not less than 80 proof. (Neutral spirits are distilled at or above 190 proof.) The straight whiskies that go into the blended whiskies are themselves distilled and aged, and there can be as many as 75 different straight whiskies and grain and neutral spirits which go into one particular blended whiskey. Blended whiskey may be served with: tonic, cola, 7-up or lemonade, dry ginger ale, soda or mineral water.

LEGBENDER COCKTAIL

30 ml (1 fl oz) blended Whiskey
30 ml (1 fl oz) Stock sweet vermouth
30 ml (1 fl oz) Stock dry vermouth
dash of Angostura bitters
ice
maraschino cherry

Pour ingredients into a mixing glass with ice, stir and strain into a cocktail glass then add a cherry.

JAPANESE WHISKY

Suntory's fourteen whiskies are widely recognized for their full, rich flavours. These blended whiskies have quickly become and have remained the pride of Japan. They are becoming increasingly popular in many other lands as well. The reasons for this phenomenal success are to be found in Suntory's excellent combination of ideal natural conditions with the application of modern technology and the company's traditional devotion to quality in distilling its whisky.

RISING SUN

60 ml (2 fl oz) Suntory whisky
15 ml (1/2 fl oz) lime or lemon juice
15 ml (1/2 fl oz) Galliano
30 ml (1 fl oz) cherry brandy
7-Up or lemonade
ice
ring of orange
maraschino cherry

Japan is blessed with numerous artesian wells that produce sparkling, pure water. From the very beginning, Suntory followed the example of the builders of Japan's ancient ritual tea houses by erecting its distilleries next to the finest of these wells. Suntory's first distillery was founded in the Yamazaki Valley in 1923.

Reflecting the company's steady growth, the need soon arose for a second distillery. After five years of searching, an equally suitable location was discovered in the Hakushu region at the foot of the Japan Alps. The new distillery was opened in 1973 and with 24 pot stills under one roof, is the world's largest malt whisky distillery. Using the finest water Japan has to offer, Suntory uses only the best barley available. The mash is distilled twice in copper pot stills before being aged to maturity in sherry-cured, white oak casks imported from North America. Malt whisky is then shipped to eight bottling plants near major Japanese cities as well as to those in Mexico, Brazil, the Philippines, Thailand and Bulgaria. The final result is a premium quality whisky which has been favourably compared to the finest Scotch whiskies.

Japanese whisky may be served with: soda water, water, mineral water, cola, 7-up or lemonade and dry ginger ale.

In a highball glass with ice pour Suntory whisky, lime or lemon juice, and Galliano. Top up with 7-Up or lemonade then float cherry brandy on top. Garnish with a ring of orange and a cherry.

AUSTRALIAN WHISKY

It is nearly one hundred years since whisky was first distilled in Australia, but it was not until shortly before World War II that large modern distilleries were established in this country. Australian distilling methods are similar to those used in the United Kingdom but the difference in Australian whisky is due to the locally grown cereal grains, climatic conditions and maturation. Australian whisky is aged in oak casks for more than five years. As standards of quality control and government regulations are very strict, Australians get whisky with a unique flavour and a product equal to that of other countries.
Australian whisky may be served with: soda water, cola, 7-up or lemonade, dry ginger ale, mineral water or water.

KINGS CROSS COCKTAIL

30 ml (1 fl oz) Australian Whisky
60 ml (2 fl oz) Baileys Irish Cream
ice

Serve in an old-fashioned glass over ice.

BOND 7 AND JAMES

Created by Eddie Tirado

60 ml (2 fl oz) Australian whisky
1 dash sweet vermouth
mineral water
orange peel
maraschino cherry

Pour whisky into a highball glass, add vermouth and top up with mineral water. Serve with garnish of orange peel and cherry.

MY MATE

60 ml (2 fl oz) Australian whisky
15 ml (1/2 fl oz) green ginger wine
dry ginger ale
ice
slice of lemon

In a highball glass with ice pour whisky and green ginger wine then top up with dry ginger ale. Garnish with a slice of lemon.

SWEET FANNY COCKTAIL

30 ml (1 fl oz) Australian whisky
30 ml (1 fl oz) cherry brandy
15 ml (1/2 fl oz) lemon juice
8 ml (1/4 fl oz) Grenadine
dash of egg white
ice

Shake or blend with ice and strain into a cocktail glass.

COBBER COCKTAIL

45 ml (1 1/2 fl oz) Australian whisky
45 ml (1 1/2 fl oz) Cinzano Bianco vermouth
ice
twist of lemon

Stir in a mixing glass with ice and strain into a cocktail glass. Garnish with a twist of lemon.

GREEN & GOLD COCKTAIL

30 ml (1 fl oz) Australian whisky
15 ml (1/2 fl oz) Galliano
15 ml (1/2 fl oz) green crème de menthe
dash of egg white
ice
green cherry
twist of lemon

Shake with ice and strain into a sour glass. Garnish with a green cherry and a twist of lemon.

YOUR SHOUT HIGHBALL

30 ml (1 fl oz) Australian Whisky
Australian beer
ice

In a highball glass pour whisky over ice and top up with beer.

CAPTAIN COOK'S ENDEAVOUR

30 ml (1 fl oz) Australian whisky
15 ml (1/2 fl oz) lemon juice
45 ml (1 1/2 fl oz) blue curaçao
few drops egg white
1 teaspoon sugar

Shake whisky, lemon juice, blue caraçao, egg white and sugar and pour into a tall glass with ice. Garnish with a sprig of mint, slice of lemon and cherry and top with lemonade.

HOT FLASHES

Created by Eddie Tirado

60 ml (2 fl oz) Australian whisky
15 ml (1/2 oz) Campari
8 ml (1/4 oz) bianco vermouth
ice
lemon peel

Mix whisky, Campari and vermouth with ice in a mixing glass. Serve with lemon peel in a cocktail glass.

BOOMERANG COCKTAIL

30 ml (1 fl oz) Australian whisky
23 ml (3/4 fl oz) dry vermouth
2 dashes lemon juice
23 ml (3/4 fl oz) Swedish Punsch

Shake ingredients with ice, then strain into a cocktail glass.

SUNTORY SOUR

juice of ¹/₂ lemon
¹/₂ teaspoon sugar
60 ml (2 fl oz) Suntory whisky
ice
soda water
¹/₂ slice orange
maraschino cherry

Shake the lemon juice, sugar, whisky and ice.
Strain into a sour glass.
Top up if desired with soda water.
Garnish with orange and cherry and serve.

SUNTORY LADY

30 ml (1 fl oz) lemon juice
1 teaspoon sugar and dash egg white
45 ml (1¹/₂ fl oz) whisky
60 ml (2 fl oz) Midori liqueur
slice of lemon and cherry

Shake and serve ingredients in a whisky sour glass. Top up with a splash of soda water and garnish with a slice of lemon and a cherry.

SUNTORY HIGHBALL

ice
2 dashes bitters
60 ml (2 fl oz) Suntory whisky
soda water or dry ginger ale
twist of lemon

Place ice in a highball glass.
Add bitters and whisky.
Fill with soda water or dry ginger ale.
Garnish with a twist of lemon and serve.

BRANDY

BRANDY BASED DRINKS

Brandy is a distillate or a mixture of distillates obtained solely from the fermented juice or mash of grapes. If made from any other fruit, it must clearly state on the label the fruit from which it is derived, e.g. peach brandy or cherry brandy. These fruit brandies are becoming increasingly popular as they are widely used in cocktails and mixed drinks.

Brandies are aged in oak casks for a minimum of two years and the usual ageing period is from three to eight years.

Brandy is produced in many countries, including Australia, but Cognac is only produced in the French district of Charente, in which the city of Cognac is situated. In order to be labelled Cognac, the grapes must be grown, fermented, and distilled in this area where there are seven 'districts', listed below in order quality.

Grande Champagne
Petite Champagne
Borderies
Fins Bois
Bons Bois
Bois Ordinaire
Bois à Terrior

The brandies from these ranges are distilled and matured separately and then blended.

Quality markings of cognac are:

* One Star
** Two Stars
*** Three Stars
V.O. Very old
V.O.P. Very old pale
V.S.O. Very superior old
V.S.O.P. Very superior old pale

Another worthy French brandy is Armagnac which comes from the region of that name in the south-west of France. Armagnac is fuller bodied and drier than Cognac.

It is best to use the younger brandies for mixed drinks. The more mature and expensive brandies are better appreciated when drunk neat; however, if your pocket is large enough you can use them for mixing.

JOAN OF ARC

30 ml (1 fl oz) brandy or Cognac
8 ml (¼ fl oz) coconut juice
8 ml (¼ fl oz) orange juice
15 ml (½ fl oz) cream .
30 ml (1 fl oz) Grand Marnier
ice

Pour the brandy into a champagne glass and flame. Shake the coconut juice, orange juice, cream and Grand Marnier in a cocktail shaker with ice then pour it over the flamed brandy.

KINGS CROSS NUT

Created by Eddie Tirado

1 coconut
3 cubes ice
60 ml (2 fl oz) brandy
30 ml (1 fl oz) Tia Maria
nutmeg

Take the top off the coconut and remove the milk. Place half the milk and ice cubes into a cocktail shaker.
Add the brandy and Tia Maria.
Shake and strain the mixture back into the coconut.
Dust with nutmeg.
Serve with a spoon and drinking straws.

COFFEE COCKTAIL

30 ml (1 fl oz) brandy
30 ml (1 fl oz) port wine
dash curaçao
yolk of 1 egg
1 teaspoon sugar
ice
nutmeg

Shake brandy, port wine, curaçao, egg yolk and sugar with ice.
Strain into a 120 ml (4 fl oz) glass.
Sprinkle nutmeg on top and serve.

BOMBAY COCKTAIL

60 ml (2 fl oz) brandy
8 ml (¼ fl oz) sweet vermouth
8 ml (¼ fl oz) dry vermouth
3 dashes curaçao
ice

Shake brandy, sweet and dry vermouth and curaçao with ice.
Strain into a cocktail glass and serve.

LEVIATHAN COCKTAIL

½ brandy
¼ sweet vermouth
¼ orange juice
ice

Shake brandy, vermouth and orange juice with ice. Pour into a cocktail glass and serve.

SIDECAR

¹/₂ brandy
¹/₄ Cointreau
¹/₄ lemon juice
ice

Shake brandy, Cointreau and lemon juice with ice. Strain into a cocktail glass and serve.

STINGER

²/₃ brandy
¹/₃ white crème de menthe
ice

Mix brandy and crème de menthe in mixing glass with ice. Serve in a cocktail glass.

BETSY ROSS

30 ml (1 fl oz) brandy
30 ml (1 fl oz) port
8 ml (¹/₄ fl oz) Cointreau
ice

Shake with ice and strain into a cocktail glass.

SOUTHERLY BUSTER

2 cubes ice
30 ml (1 fl oz) brandy
15 ml (¹/₂ fl oz) dry vermouth
15 ml (¹/₂ fl oz) lime cordial
dry ginger ale
slice lemon

In a highball glass add ice, brandy, vermouth and lime cordial.
Fill up with dry ginger ale.
Serve with drinking straws and a slice of lemon.

BRANDY LIME AND SODA

45 ml (1¹/₂ fl oz) brandy
15 ml (¹/₂ fl oz) lime juice
soda water
ice
slice of lemon

Top brandy and lime juice with soda water and ice. Serve in a tall glass and garnish with slice of lemon.

BULL FROG

60 ml (2 fl oz) brandy
30 ml (1 fl oz) lime juice
dash of egg white
ice

Shake with ice and strain into a cocktail glass.

MATILDA

30 ml (1 fl oz) brandy
30 ml (1 fl oz) cream
30 ml (1 fl oz) Kahlua
ice

Shake with ice and strain into a cocktail glass.

APPLE JACK

60 ml (2 fl oz) brandy
apple juice
ice

Pour brandy into a goblet with ice and top up with apple juice.

BRANDY BUSTER

60 ml (2 fl oz) brandy
30 ml (1 fl oz) cherry brandy
30 ml (1 fl oz) advokaat
60 ml (2 fl oz) cream
ice

Blend with ice and serve in a champagne glass.

Some very popular brandy drinks are:
30 ml (1 fl oz) brandy over ice topped with soda water, brandy with dry ginger ale, brandy with lemonade, brandy with cola and brandy with orange juice.

AMERICAN BEAUTY COCKTAIL

15 ml (¹/₂ fl oz) brandy
15 ml (¹/₂ fl oz) dry vermouth
3 dashes white crème de menthe
15 ml (¹/₂ fl oz) grenadine
15 ml (¹/₂ fl oz) orange juice
port wine
ice

Shake brandy, dry vermouth, crème de menthe, grenadine and orange juice with ice.
Strain into a cocktail glass.
Top with port wine and serve.

HORSE'S NECK

2 dashes Angostura bitters
dry ginger ale
45 ml (1¹/₂ fl oz) brandy
lemon
4 cubes ice

Peel the skin of a lemon in one piece. Place one end of the peel over the edge of a high- ball glass (giving the effect of a horse's neck).
Fill the glass with ice cubes.
Add brandy and bitters.
Top with dry ginger ale and serve.

BRANDY ALEXANDER

¹/₃ brandy
¹/₃ crème de cacao
¹/₃ fresh cream
nutmeg

Shake brandy, crème de cacao and fresh cream with ice.
Strain into a champagne glass.
Serve with nutmeg sprinkled on top.

BOSOM CARESSER

²/₃ brandy
¹/₃ orange curaçao
yolk of 1 egg
1 teaspoon grenadine

Shake brandy, curaçao, egg yolk and grenadine.
Pour into a cocktail glass and serve.

JACK-IN-THE BOX

¹/₂ applejack brandy
¹/₂ pineapple juice
dash Angostura bitters
ice

Shake brandy, pineapple juice and bitters with
ice. Pour into a cocktail glass and serve.

DEVIL COCKTAIL

40 ml (1¹/₃ fl oz) brandy
40 ml (1¹/₃ fl oz) green crème de menthe

Stir brandy and crème de menthe.
Strain into a cocktail glass and serve.

Gin

GIN BASED DRINKS

Gin was first produced in Holland in the seventeenth century
as a medicinal beverage due to the presence of the juniper berry,
which is one of main flavourings necessary for the production of gin.
There are two processes for making gin – distilled and compound gins.
Nearly all brands are distilled. Compound gin is a simple process that
mixes neutral spirits with the juniper berries.

Distilled gin is obtained by original distillation of mash or by the redistillation of distilled spirits, over or with juniper berries and other plants. The grain formula consists of 75 percent corn, 15 percent barley malt and 10 percent other grains, and the resulting spirit has to be mixed with distilled water as it is too strong to drink. As the water differs from country to country, so does the gin. Each distiller has his own secret formula which in some cases has not altered since the first distiller made gin.

Most brands use the word 'dry' and even 'London dry' on their labels. This means that the gin lacks sweetness and any pronounced aromatic flavour or bouquet. 'London dry' originally applied to gin produced near London but is now descriptive of many gins of today. Gin does not have to be aged.

There are several kinds of gin. Although 'London dry' is the most commonly used there are others not at all alike in flavour. Tom gin is a slightly more perfumed and sweeter gin; Golden gin is a dry gin and because it is aged is gold or straw-coloured (but the distiller by law cannot make any age claim); Plymouth gin is the driest of all and is produced by one distiller only; the sweetest is Sloe gin, a mixture of dry gin and sloe berries; Dutch gin which is sold under the name of 'Geneva' or 'Holland' and distilled in Holland differs from English gins in that it is heavy in body and very aromatic.

Some very popular gin drinks are:
30 ml (1 fl oz) gin over ice and topped with tonic water, gin with bitter lemon, gin with lemonade, gin with cola, gin with lemon squash, gin with lime and soda water and gin with mineral water.

NAPOLEON COCKTAIL

45 ml (1 1/2 fl oz) dry gin
dash Fernet Branca
dash Dubonnet
dash curaçao
cracked ice

Stir gin, Fernet Branca, Dubonnet and curaçao with ice.
Serve in a cocktail glass.

GIN TROPICAL

30 ml (1 fl oz) Gordon's gin
30 ml (1 fl oz) passionfruit syrup
15 ml (1/2 fl oz) Bols blue curaçao
soda water
maraschino cherry
slice of orange

Shake gin, passionfruit syrup and curaçao.
Strain into a glass and top with soda water.
Serve with drinking straws, cherry and a slice of orange for garnish.

ROLLS ROYCE

30 ml (1 fl oz) gin
15 ml (1/2 fl oz) dry vermouth
15 ml (1/2 fl oz) sweet vermouth
8 ml (1/4 fl oz) Benedictine
cracked ice

Stir gin, dry and sweet vermouth and Benedictine with ice.
Strain into a cocktail glass and serve.

SINGAPORE SLING

45 ml (1 1/2 fl oz) gin
dash Benedictine
23 ml (3/4 fl oz) cherry brandy
juice of 1/2 lemon
dash Angostura bitters
slice of orange
cherry

Shake over ice and serve in a highball glass.
Garnish with a slice of orange and cherry.

SHERRY COCKTAIL

30 ml (1 fl oz) gin
30 ml (1 fl oz) sweet sherry
30 ml (1 fl oz) lemon juice

Shake gin, sherry and lemon juice.
Strain into a cocktail glass and serve.

PINK LADY NO. 1

4 dashes grenadine
4 dashes applejack brandy
60 ml (2 fl oz) dry gin
4 dashes fresh cream
ice

Shake grenadine, applejack, gin and cream with ice. Strain into a champagne glass and serve.

PINK LADY NO. 2

4 dashes grenadine
60 ml (2 fl oz) gin
1 dash egg white

Shake grenadine, gin and egg white. Strain into a cocktail glass and serve.

FRENCH 75

45 ml (1 1/2 fl oz) dry gin
1 teaspoon caster (powdered) sugar
juice of 1/2 lemon
cracked ice
90 ml (3 fl oz) champagne
twist lemon

Combine gin, sugar and lemon juice, and shake with ice.
Pour into a highball glass.
Fill glass with champagne and add a twist of lemon to serve.
Note: Do not stir or champagne will lose its efferverscence.

ORANGE BLOSSOM COCKTAIL

30 ml (1 fl oz) gin
60 ml (2 fl oz) orange juice
cracked ice

Shake gin and orange juice with ice. Strain into a cocktail glass and serve.

ELEPHANT WALK

cracked ice
30 ml (1 fl oz) dry gin
15 ml (1/2 fl oz) tequila
15 ml (1/2 fl oz) fresh orange juice
dash grenadine
dash Angostura bitters
1/2 slice orange
1/2 slice lemon
5 cm (2 inch) stick of cucumber

Fill an old-fashioned glass with cracked ice.
Add gin, tequila, orange juice, grenadine and bitters.
Garnish with orange, lemon and cucumber.
Add a swizzle stick and serve.

WHITE LADY

30 ml (1 fl oz) gin
15 ml (1 fl oz) Cointreau
juice of 1/2 lemon
dash of egg white
ice

Shake and strain with ice.
Serve in a cocktail glass.

VIRGIN COCKTAIL

30 ml (1 fl oz) dry gin
23 ml (3/4 fl oz) white crème de menthe
23 ml (3/4 oz) Forbidden Fruit
maraschino cherry

Shake gin, crème de menthe and Forbidden Fruit. Strain and serve with cherry in a cocktail glass.

CORONATION COCKTAIL

15 ml (1/2 fl oz) dry gin
15 ml (1/2 fl oz) Dubonnet
15 ml (1/2 fl oz) dry vermouth
cracked ice

Stir gin, Dubonnet and vermouth with ice. Strain into a cocktail glass and serve.

APRICOT COCKTAIL

30 ml (1 fl oz) gin
15 ml (1/2 fl oz) apricot brandy
1/2 teaspoon grenadine
2 drops bitters
1/4 teaspoon lemon juice
cracked ice

Shake gin, apricot brandy, grenadine, bitters and lemon juice with ice.
Strain into a cocktail glass and serve.

ALASKA COCKTAIL

60 ml (2 fl oz) gin
23 ml (³/4 fl oz) Yellow Chartreuse
ice
lemon peel

Stir gin and Yellow Chartreuse with ice.
Strain into a cocktail glass.
Twist a lemon peel over the top and serve.

PERFECT COCKTAIL

45 ml (1 ¹/2 fl oz) dry gin
23 ml (³/4 fl oz) dry vermouth
23 ml (³/4 fl oz) sweet vermouth

Stir gin, dry and sweet vermouth.
Serve in a cocktail glass.

KOOKABURRA COCKTAIL

30 ml (1 fl oz) gin
60 ml (2 fl oz) green crème de menthe
ice

Serve over ice in an old-fashioned glass.

MAYFAIR

30 ml (1 fl oz) Beefeater gin
15 ml (¹/2 fl oz) apricot brandy
60 ml (2 fl oz) orange juice
ice

Shake with ice and strain into a cocktail glass.

GIBSON DRY

23 ml (³/4 fl oz) gin
23 ml (³/4 fl oz) dry vermouth
cracked ice
pickled onion

Stir gin and vermouth with ice.
Strain into a chilled cocktail glass and garnish with an onion.

GIBSON SWEET

23 ml (³/4 fl oz) gin
23 ml (³/4 fl oz) sweet vermouth
pickled onion
cracked ice

Stir gin and vermouth with ice.
Strain into a chilled cocktail glass and garnish with an onion.

WATERMELON COCKTAIL

60 ml (2 fl oz) watermelon juice
45 ml (1 ¹/2 fl oz) gin
ice

Pour the watermelon juice and gin over ice and strain into a champagne glass.

WHITE LIGHTNING

45 ml (1 ¹/2 fl oz) gin
15 ml (¹/2 fl oz) Cointreau
15 ml (¹/2 fl oz) white crème de menthe
ice
twist of lemon
mint leaf

Stir over ice and strain into a cocktail glass. Garnish with a twist of lemon and a mint leaf.

O'BRIEN PUNCH COCKTAIL

30 ml (1 fl oz) gin
30 ml (1 fl oz) Mount Gay Barbados rum
60 ml (2 fl oz) guava juice
ice

Shake with ice and strain into a cocktail glass.

GEORGIE

30 ml (1 fl oz) gin
60 ml (2 fl oz) Vaccari cream liqueur
ice

Serve over ice in an old-fashioned glass.

FORT APACHE COCKTAIL

45 ml (1 ¹/2 fl oz) Mohawk gin
30 ml (1 fl oz) lime juice
dash of grenadine
dash of egg white
ice

Shake with ice and strain into a cocktail glass.

SWEET NOLLY COCKTAIL

30 ml (1 fl oz) gin
60 ml (2 fl oz) Noilly Prat sweet vermouth
dash of Angostura bitters
ice
maraschino cherry

Stir in a mixing glass with ice and strain into a cocktail glass. Garnish with a cherry.

MOHAWK COOLER

60 ml (2 fl oz) Mohawk gin
30 ml (1 fl oz) green crème de menthe
8 ml (1/4 fl oz) lime or lemon juice
ice
7-Up or Lemonade
mint
slice of lime or lemon

Pour into a highball glass with ice and top up with 7-Up or Lemonade. Garnish with mint and a slice of lime or lemon.

BRONX COCKTAIL

30 ml (1 fl oz) dry gin
15 ml (1/2 fl oz) orange juice
dash dry vermouth
dash sweet vermouth
cracked ice

Shake gin, orange juice, dry and sweet vermouth with cracked ice.
Serve in a cocktail glass.

BLUE MOON COCKTAIL

30 ml (1 fl oz) dry gin
15 ml (1/2 fl oz) Crème Yvette
15 ml (1/2 fl oz) lemon juice
cracked ice

Stir gin, Crème Yvette and lemon juice with ice. Strain into a cocktail glass and serve.

NEW YORKER COCKTAIL

15 ml (1/2 fl oz) gin
45 ml (1 1/2 fl oz) dry vermouth
15 ml (1/2 fl oz) dry sherry
dash Cointreau
cracked ice

Stir gin, vermouth, sherry and Cointreau with ice.
Serve in a cocktail glass.

ALEXANDER COCKTAIL

45 ml (1 1/2 fl oz) gin
23 ml (3/4 fl oz) crème de cacao
15 ml (1/2 fl oz) fresh cream
ice
nutmeg

Shake gin, crème de cacao and cream with ice.
Strain into a cocktail glass.
Sprinkle nutmeg on top and serve.

ABBEY COCKTAIL

60 ml (2 fl oz) gin
30 ml (1 fl oz) orange juice
dash Angostura bitters
dash sweet vermouth
cracked ice
maraschino cherry

Shake gin, orange juice, bitters and vermouth with ice.
Strain into a cocktail glass.
Serve with a cherry.

GILROY COCKTAIL

15 ml (1/2 fl oz) gin
15 ml (1/2 fl oz) cherry brandy
8 ml (1/4 fl oz) lemon juice
8 ml (1/4 fl oz) dry vermouth
dash orange bitters
cracked ice

Shake gin, cherry brandy, lemon juice, vermouth and bitters with ice.
Strain into a cocktail glass and serve.

AMSTERDAM COCKTAIL

30 ml (1 fl oz) Holland gin
15 ml (1/2 fl oz) orange juice
15 ml (1/2 fl oz) Cointreau
4 dashes orange bitters
cracked ice

Shake gin, orange juice, Cointreau and bitters with ice.
Strain into a cocktail glass and serve.

MARTINI (DRY)

Eddie's recommended recipe.

cube ice
75 ml (2 1/2 fl oz) dry gin
15 ml (1/2 fl oz) dry vermouth
olive or a twist of lemon

Into a martini mixing glass filled with cube ice gently pour the gin.
Add vermouth. Stir very gently clockwise.
Strain and serve in a cocktail glass with an olive or a twist of lemon. The earliest records show the Martini recipe to consist of:

1/2 gin and 1/2 dry vermouth
dash orange bitters (to make it extra dry)
dash Angostura bitters

Today with American influence, the extra dry Martini has been introduced into Australia. It is not unusual to mix a Dry Martini 10 parts gin to 1 part vermouth. We have also known the bartender to just wave the vermouth cork over the gin or spray on the vermouth with an atomiser.

CLOVER CLUB COCKTAIL

45 ml (1 1/2 fl oz) dry gin
4 dashes grenadine
juice of 1/2 lemon and 1 egg white

Shake ingredients with ice. Serve in a champagne glass.

MARTINI (SWEET)

ice
60 ml (2 fl oz) gin
30 ml (1 fl oz) sweet vermouth
maraschino cherry

Put ice into a martini glass.
Pour over the gin, add vermouth and stir very gently clockwise.
Serve with a cherry.

PINK GIN

3 dashes Angostura bitters
2 cubes ice
45 ml (1 1/2 fl oz) gin
30 ml (1 fl oz) water

In a goblet put 3 dashes bitters. Rotate in a glass. Throw out the bitters. Add ice cubes, gin and water, and serve.

QUEEN'S COCKTAIL

1 part dry gin
1 part dry vermouth
1 part sweet vermouth
1 part pineapple juice
maraschino cherry
small piece of pineapple for garnish

Shake gin, dry and sweet vermouth and pineapple juice.
Serve in a cocktail glass with pineapple and cherry.

FALLEN ANGEL COCKTAIL

45 ml (1 1/2 fl oz) gin
2 dashes green crème de menthe
juice of 1/2 lemon
cracked ice
dash Angostura bitters

Shake gin, crème de menthe, bitters, and lemon juice with ice.
Strain into a 90 ml (3 fl oz) cocktail glass and serve.
Note: In New Zealand, a Fallen Angel Cocktail consists of 30 ml (1 fl oz) Advokaat and 30 ml (1 fl oz) Cherry Brandy topped with lemonade and ginger ale served in a highball glass.

Rum

RUM BASED DRINKS

'Rumbullion' meaning 'rumpus' was the drink of the slaves on plantations in the British West Indies as early as the seventeenth century, and from this came the drink we know today as rum. Rum is made basically of sugar cane by-products and is produced in most sugar-growing countries. Puerto Rico is a big rum producer, and other suppliers are British West Indies, Venezuela, Brazil, Jamaica and Australia.

It is the amount of burnt sugar cane syrup, or caramel, that gives colour and flavour to the drink and rum comes in a range of colours and flavours: there are three main types – white, gold and black label. Puerto Rican rums are blends of aged rums distilled at a high proof for lightness and dryness and aged from one to three years. White and gold labels are produced there, the gold being sweeter and darker than the white. The Jamaicans produce gold and black label, the black being richer, darker and more heavy-bodied than the gold. These are aged in oak casks.

FROZEN DAIQUIRI

Follow the recipe given for Daiquiri; serve in a champagne glass with shaved ice and two short straws. Add 1 dash maraschino (optional).

HOT BUTTERED RUM

45 ml (1 1/2 fl oz) Jamaican rum
1 lump sugar
small slice butter
boiling water
nutmeg

Use an old-fashioned glass or mug.
Combine the rum, sugar and butter.
Fill the glass with boiling water over a silver spoon (to prevent glass breaking) and stir.
Sprinkle nutmeg on top and serve.

PLANTER'S PUNCH

60 ml (2 fl oz) Jamaican rum
30 ml (1 fl oz) lemon or lime juice
dash Angostura bitters
1 teaspoon grenadine
ice
soda water
lemon, orange slices
maraschino cherry

Place rum, lemon or lime juice, bitters and grenadine in a highball glass with ice.
Top with soda water and serve with straws.
Garnish with a slice of lemon or orange and cherry.

PABLO

cracked ice
30 ml (1 fl oz) Bacardi
15 ml (1/2 fl oz) Cointreau
15 ml (1/2 fl oz) Bols advokaat
30 ml (1 oz) pineapple
maraschino cherry

Half fill cocktail shaker with ice.
Add Bacardi, Cointreau, advokaat and pineapple.
Shake and strain into a champagne glass.
Garnish with a cherry and serve.

BANANA COW

Created by Eddie Tirado

45 ml (1 1/2 fl oz) cream
30 ml (1 fl oz) white rum
30 ml (1 fl oz) crème de banana
dash of grenadine
nutmeg

Pour into a cocktail shaker with ice. Shake and strain into a cocktail glass. Sprinkle nutmeg on top and serve.

GOLDEN SLIPPER

30 ml (1 fl oz) Galliano
30 ml (1 fl oz) Bacardi
champagne
strawberries

In a mixing glass, stir Galliano and Bacardi with ice. Strain into a tulip champagne glass and garnish with strawberries.

BLUE HAWAII

45 ml (1¹/₂ fl oz) white rum
30 ml (1 fl oz) sweet and sour mix
45 ml (1¹/₂ fl oz) blue curaçao
150 ml (5 fl oz) pineapple juice
pineapple wedge
cherry

Shake with ice and pour into a tall glass. Garnish with a pineapple wedge and a cherry.

ZOMBIE

the original version

60 ml (2 fl oz) light rum
30 ml (1 fl oz) Jamaican rum
15 ml (¹/₂ fl oz) apricot brandy
¹/₂ teaspoon caster (powdered) sugar
15 ml (¹/₂ fl oz) lemon juice
1 bar spoon (or 1 teaspoon) papaya nectar
and/or 1 bar spoon pineapple juice and/or
1 bar spoon passionfruit juice and/or
1 bar spoon plum or apricot juice
cracked ice
mint, pineapple, cherry for garnish
15 ml (¹/₂ fl oz) 150 proof Demarara rum
(if available)

In a cocktail shaker put all the above ingredients, except the Demarara rum. Shake well with cracked ice.
Pour unstrained into a zombie glass which is half-full of cracked ice.
Decorate with a sprig of mint or a pineapple spear and cherry.
Top with Demarara rum, pouring carefully so that it floats on the surface of the drink.
Serve with drinking straws.

MAI TAI (VARIATION)

60 ml (2 fl oz) dark Jamaican rum
juice of ¹/₂ lime or lemon
15 ml (1¹/₂ fl oz) apricot or regular brandy
15 ml (¹/₂ fl oz) white or orange curaçao
slice of pineapple

Combine all ingredients and shake.
Strain and pour into an old-fashioned or highball glass.
Garnish with a slice of pineapple.

KING'S DAIQUIRI

Created by Eddie Tirado

15 ml (¹/₂ fl oz) lemon juice
15 ml (¹/₂ fl oz) Parfait Amour
45 ml (1¹/₂ oz) Bacardi
¹/₄ teaspoon sugar
dash egg white

Blend lemon juice, Parfait Amour, Bacardi, sugar and egg white. Serve in a champagne glass.

SKI-LIFT

45 ml (1¹/₂ fl oz) Bacardi rum
30 ml (1 fl oz) coconut milk
30 ml (1 fl oz) cream
15 ml (¹/₂ fl oz) white crème de cacao
15 ml (¹/₂ fl oz) Sambuca di Galliano
ice
2 strips lemon peel

Shake or blend with ice and serve in a champagne glass. Garnish with lemon peel.

ROMANTICO

60 ml (2 fl oz) Vaccari cream liqueur
30 ml (1 fl oz) Bacardi rum
ice

Serve in a champagne glass over ice.

GAY CHI-CHI

60 ml (2 fl oz) Mount Gay rum
30 ml (1 fl oz) coconut milk
30 ml (1 fl oz) cream
30 ml (1 fl oz) pineapple juice
ice

Shake or blend with ice and serve in a goblet.

Popular Rum Drinks include:
Rum with strawberries and cream; Rum with bananas and cream; Rum with cola, soda water, tonic water, dry ginger ale, bitter lemon, lemon squash, 7-up or lemonade, lime and mineral water.

A more exotic cocktail can be created as follows: In an electric blender add 60 ml (2 fl oz) rum with fresh strawberries and cream or bananas and cream and blend with ice. Strain into a champagne glass and garnish with strawberries or bananas.

MAI TAI

60 ml (2 fl oz) light rum
30 ml (1 fl oz) Jamaican rum
1 teaspoon sugar
15 ml (1/2 fl oz) lemon or lime juice
15 ml (1/2 fl oz) almond liqueur
crushed ice
sprig of mint
pineapple spear
maraschino cherry

Pour light and Jamaican rum, sugar, lemon or lime juice and almond liqueur into an old-fashioned glass half filled with ice. Mix well.
Add crushed ice to fill and stir gently to combine the ice with other ingredients.
Garnish with a sprig of mint, a pineapple spear and a maraschino cherry. If Mai Tai mix is available just add spirit.

PINA COLADA

45 ml (1 1/2 fl oz) white rum
30 ml (1 fl oz) pineapple juice
30 ml (1 fl oz) coconut milk
15 ml (1/2 fl oz) cream
15 ml (1/2 fl oz) Cointreau
ice
slice of pineapple
cherry

Shake with ice, strain into champagne glass and garnish with slice of pineapple and cherry.

HAWAIIAN HONEYMOON

45 ml (1 1/2 fl oz) Bacardi
60 ml (2 fl oz) orange juice
30 ml (2 fl oz) pineapple juice
dash lemon juice
dash grenadine
Pernod 45
cherry, pineapple and orange for garnish

Mix Bacardi, orange juice, pineapple juice, lemon juice and grenadine. Float Pernod 45 on top. Garnish with a cherry, a slice of pineapple and orange, and serve.

ZOMBIE

30 ml (1 fl oz) lemon or lime juice
4 dashes passionola or papaya juice
4 dashes each of apricot and cherry brandy
30 ml (1 fl oz) each of white, dark and Jamaican rum
151 proof rum
green and red cherries and slice of orange

Fill a zombie glass with cracked ice. Add the above ingredients, except 151 proof rum, and stir. Top with 151 proof rum. Garnish with cherries and a slice of orange.

DAIQUIRI

3 parts Bacardi (white)
1 part lemon or lime juice
3 dashes of Gomme Syrup or
1 teaspoon sugar

Thoroughly shake Bacardi, lemon or lime juice, Gomme Syrup or sugar. Strain into a chilled cocktail glass and serve.

BACARDI COCKTAIL

3 parts Bacardi (white)
1 part lemon juice
dash grenadine
dash egg white
maraschino cherry

Shake Bacardi, lemon juice, grenadine and egg white.
Strain into a cocktail glass.
Garnish with a cherry on a toothpick and serve.

VODKA

VODKA BASED DRINKS

Vodka was produced in Poland in the twelfth century and has been a favourite drink in Russia and Poland ever since. It is an alcoholic distillate from a fermented mash of grain. In the making of vodka as we know it in Australia, nothing is added to the neutral spirits; all character is removed leaving it odourless, tasteless, colourless and smooth. This is a distinct advantage, for it may then be added as a fillip to a favourite non-alcoholic beverage. However because the flavour of vodka is not immediately discernible in vodka-mixed drinks, the uninitiated may unintentionally over-imbibe – with 'disastrous' results. In Europe, however, vodka is flavoured and is drunk chilled and neat. It does not need to be aged. Vodka may be served with: water, cola, lemonade or 7-up, ginger ale, and mineral water. A popular drink is 30 ml (1 fl oz) vodka over ice, topped up with your favourite fruit juice.

BREATHALISER BUSTER

¹/₃ crème de menthe
¹/₃ Cointreau
¹/₃ vodka

Serve the above ingredients in a cocktail glass.

ROYAL SNOWBALL

30 ml (1 fl oz) vodka
30 ml (1 fl oz) Advokaat
30 ml (1 fl oz) whipped cream
jelly crystals
ice
7-Up or Lemonade
1 marshmallow

Crust the rim of a highball glass's with jelly crystals. Pour vodka, Advokaat and whipped cream over ice then top up with 7-Up or lemonade. Garnish with marshmallow.

PINEAPPLE DELIGHT

¹/₃ unsweetened pineapple juice
¹/₃ vodka
¹/₃ white curaçao
ice
¹/₄ slice pineapple

Shake pineapple, vodka and curaçao with ice. Pour into a champagne glass with ¼ slice of pineapple and serve.

THREE ORBIT

Created by Eddie Tirado

1 part Drambuie
1 part Cointreau
1 part vodka

Shake Drambuie, Cointreau and vodka. Strain and serve.

SALTY DOG

3 cubes ice
45 ml (1 ¹/₂ fl oz) vodka
grapefruit juice

In a highball glass place ice and vodka. Top up with grapefruit juice and serve.

SCREWDRIVER

2 cubes ice
45 ml (1 ¹/₂ fl oz) vodka
orange juice
slice of orange
maraschino cherry

In a highball glass place ice and vodka. Top up with orange juice. Garnish with a slice of orange and a cherry and serve.

PINK ELEPHANT

cracked ice
23 ml (³/₄ fl oz) vodka
23 ml (³/₄ fl oz) Galliano
23 ml (³/₄ fl oz) Crème de Noyeau
or almond liqueur
23 ml (³/₄ fl oz) fresh orange juice
23 ml (³/₄ fl oz) fresh cream
dash grenadine
cinnamon

Half fill a cocktail shaker with ice. Shake all the ingredients. Strain into a champagne glass. Sprinkle cinnamon on top and serve.

MOSCOW MULE

3 cubes ice
60 ml (2 fl oz) vodka
30 ml (1 fl oz) lemon juice
ginger beer
mint

In a highball glass put 3 cubes ice; add vodka and lemon juice.
Fill with ginger beer.
Garnish with mint and serve.

VODKA MIST

45 ml (1 1/2 fl oz) vodka
twist of lemon

In a cocktail shaker pour vodka, add twist of lemon.
Serve unstrained in an old-fashioned glass.

CHOCOLATE CHERRY COCKTAIL

30 ml (1 fl oz) vodka
60 ml (2 fl oz) Cheri-Suisse liqueur
ice

Stir in a mixing glass with ice and strain into a cocktail glass.

GODMOTHER

23 ml (3/4 fl oz) Amaretto di Galliano
45 ml (1 1/2 fl oz) vodka
ice

Serve in a highball glass over ice.

SWEET CAT

30 ml (1 fl oz) Tia Maria
30 ml (1 fl oz) vodka

Stir Tia Maria and vodka in a mixing glass with ice.
Strain into a cocktail glass and float cream on top.

NEW ZEALAND BUSH

60 ml (2 fl oz) Ti-Toki liqueur
30 ml (1 fl oz) vodka
ice
mint leaf

Pour ingredients over ice into a wine glass. Garnish with a mint leaf.

VODKA ON THE ROCKS

3 cubes ice
45 ml (1 1/2 fl oz) vodka

Pour vodka over ice in an old-fashioned glass and serve.

RED SEA

30 ml (1 fl oz) vodka
30 ml (1 fl oz) Rosso Antico
8 ml (1/4 fl oz) Cointreau
ice

Stir in a mixing glass with ice and strain into a cocktail glass.

TURKISH COCKTAIL

30 ml (1 fl oz) vodka
60 ml (2 fl oz) Pasha liqueur
ice

Stir in a mixing glass with ice and strain into a cocktail glass. Pasha Liqueur is a Turkish Coffee Liqueur.

HOT SABRA

45 ml (1 1/2 fl oz) Sabra liqueur
30 ml (1 fl oz) vodka
black coffee
whipped cream

Pour Sabra liqueur and vodka into a mug. Top up with hot coffee and a spoon of whipped cream.

VODKA MARTINI

Follow recipe as for Gin Martini (page 44) but substitute vodka for gin.

BLUE WATERS

ice
15 ml (¹/₂ fl oz) vodca
30 ml (1 fl oz) blue curaçao
30 ml (1 fl oz) Galliano

Fill a highball glass with ice and add vodka, Galliano and blue curaçao. Top up with water.

BLOODY MARY

dash Worcestershire sauce
2 drops Tabasco sauce
8 ml (¹/₄ fl oz) lemon juice
salt and pepper
3 cubes ice
60 ml (2 fl oz) vodka (white rum, gin or tequila can be substituted)
tomato juice

In a highball glass put Worcestershire sauce, Tabasco sauce, lemon juice, salt and pepper. Mix together and then add ice cubes and vodka. Top with tomato juice.
Serve with swizzle stick.

RUSSIAN COCKTAIL

30 ml (1 fl oz) vodka
30 ml (1 fl oz) dry gin
30 ml (1 fl oz) crème de cacao

Stir vodka, gin and crème de cacao. Strain into a cocktail glass and serve.

MOON CRATER

Created by Eddie Tirado

30 ml (1 fl oz) vodka
30 ml (1 fl oz) advokaat
Fanta
fresh cream
nutmeg
ice
maraschino cherry

Put vodka and advokaat in a highball glass.
Fill with Fanta and top with cream.
Dust with nutmeg.
Serve with ice and garnish with cherry.

CHI-CHI COCKTAIL

45 ml (1½ fl oz) vodka
60 ml (2 fl oz) pineapple juice
(preferable sweetened)
30 ml (1 fl oz) coconut milk
15 ml (½ fl oz) Cointreau
8 ml (½ fl oz) lime or lemon juice
crushed ice
cherry
pineapple for garnish

Blend or shake ingredients with crushed ice. Serve in a champagne glass. Garnish with a cherry and a ring or piece of pineapple.

BLACK RUSSIAN

3 parts vodka
1 part Kahlua
ice

Serve vodka and Kahlua on the rocks. This can also be served with equal parts of vodka and Kahlua.

TEQUILA

Tequila dates back to Aztec times in Central America, long before the Spanish conquered the country. True tequila must come from the city of Tequila in southwest Mexico, but most tequilas imported into Australia come via the United States. Tequila is made from the sap of the wild Mescal plant (similar to cactus) and it is produced near the city of Tequila where the Mescal plants are abundant. The mescal is then fermented and distilled and becomes tequila. There are two varieties – white and gold label. The white label is not aged, whereas the gold is aged in used whisky barrels just long enough to impart the gold colour ready for bottling.

Tequila is reputed to have a very strong alcoholic content but it is much the same as gin or vodka. It probably earned its mule-kick reputation because of the way the peons (Spanish American workers) drank it. A piece of lemon and some salt were put on the clenched fist of the left hand. Tequila was drunk from the right hand followed by a lick of lemon and salt. Today the Mexicans drink tequila with their own hot version of tomato juice and call it Sangrita.

Tequila may be served with: cola, soda water, tonic water, dry ginger ale, bitter lemon, mineral water, 7-up or lemonade or your favourite juice.

PEACH MARGARITA

30 ml (1 fl oz) tequila
15 ml (1/2 fl oz) lime or lemon juice
60 ml (2 fl oz) peach juice
ice

Rim a champagne glass with salt (optional). Shake ingredients with ice and pour into glass.

TEQUILA COCKTAIL

juice of 1/2 lemon
4 dashes grenadine
60 ml (2 fl oz) tequila
dash egg white
ice
twist of lemon

Vigorously shake lemon juice, grenadine, tequila and egg white with ice.
Strain into a cocktail glass.
Serve with a twist of lemon for garnish.

P.R. COCKTAIL

60 ml (2 fl oz) Puerto Rican rum
1 large slice seedless watermelon
30 ml (1 fl oz) tequila

Blend rum and watermelon with ice in blender. Pour into a highball glass and float tequila on top.

TEQUILA STRAIGHT

45 ml (1 1/2 oz) tequila in shot glass
slice of lemon
salt

Hold the glass in your right hand, the lemon in your left hand. Place the salt on the side of your hand near the thumb. Then, lick the salt, drink the tequila, and bite into the lemon; say 'olé', and wait for the bulls to come!

HOT MARY

dash of Worcestershire sauce
2 drops Tabasco sauce
8 ml (¹/₄ fl oz) lemon or lime juice
salt and pepper
60 ml (2 fl oz) tequila
tomato juice

Take a sour glass, moisten the rim with a slice of lemon, then sprinkle salt on the rim. Pour in ingredients, then stir and garnish with a stick of celery.

MARGARITA

salt
45 ml (1¹/₂ oz) tequila
15 ml (¹/₂ oz) Triple Sec or Cointreau
30 ml (1 fl oz) fresh lemon or lime juice
slice of lemon

Rim the glass with salt by first moistening the rim with a slice of lemon; then, sprinkle salt over the moistened area.
Vigorously shake the tequila, Triple Sec or Cointreau, and lemon or lime juice.
Strain into a cocktail glass.
Garnish with a slice of lemon and serve.

TEQUILA SUNRISER

ice
60 ml (2 fl oz) tequila
orange juice
8 ml (¹/₄ fl oz) grenadine
ring of orange
cherry

In an old-fashioned glass with ice pour tequila and top up with orange juice. Float grenadine on top. Garnish with a ring of orange and a cherry.

Sake

This rice wine is the traditional Japanese drink and is usually served warm in small cups called Sakazuki and poured from a narrow-mouthed bottle called tokkuri. Its colour can vary from clear to pale amber and each brand has a distinctive character and taste. It does not need ageing.

Sake Bull-Shot

60 ml (2 fl oz) sake
1 cube of beef stock
60 ml (2 fl oz) hot water
¼ teaspoon of celery salt or salt
dash of lemon juice
ice
slice of lemon peel

Dissolve stock cube in hot water. Add celery salt then squeeze of lemon juice and sake. Stir and serve on the rocks in an old-fashioned glass. Garnish with a slice of lemon peel.

Sake Squash

60 ml (2 fl oz) sake
30 ml (1 fl oz) lemon cordial or lemon squash
dash of Angostura bitters
ice
soda water
slice of lemon

Put all ingredients in a highball glass with ice and top up with soda water or club soda. Garnish with a slice of lemon.

SAKE COCKTAIL

30 ml (1 fl oz) sake
30 ml (1 fl oz) Midori
30 ml (1 fl oz) Suntory vodka
ice
cherry

In a mixing glass stir the ingredients. Strain into a cocktail glass partly filled with ice. Garnish with a cherry.

TAMAGOZAKE COCKTAIL

180 ml (6 fl oz) sake
1 egg
1 teaspoon sugar

Bring sake to the boil in a saucepan and light with a match.
Allow to burn for 1 second.
Remove from heat.
Add egg and sugar and stir.
Pour into a drinking cup and serve.

SAKE HIGHBALL

90 ml (3 fl oz) sake
juice of ¼ lemon
1 teaspoon caster (powdered) sugar
slice of lemon

Stir sake, lemon juice and sugar with ice and top with soda water. Garnish with a slice of lemon and serve.

CHAMPAGNE

Of all the sparkling wines champagne is one of the best. Infinite care goes into bringing the bottle of champagne to the remarkable degree of perfection which justifies its high price. The bubbles of sparkling champagne are the same as the bubbles of bottled beer: they are tiny drops of liquid, disturbed, whipped and chased by escaping carbonic acid gas at the time of fermentation.

Champagne should always be served cold but not over-iced. It usually has a golden straw colour but there is also pink champagne.

A TOUCH OF MINK

15 ml (1/2 fl oz) Pernod
champagne

In a champagne glass, pour Pernod and top up with chilled champagne.

MIMOSA COCKTAIL

1/2 orange juice (chilled)
1/2 champagne (chilled)

In a champagne glass pour orange juice and champagne and serve.

JACKIE

chilled champagne
chilled peach juice

Pour into a champagne glass, 1/2 champagne and 1/2 peach juice.

MILLIONAIRE COCKTAIL

cube sugar
15 ml (1/2 fl oz) Galliano
chilled champagne
1 strawberry
sprig or mint

In a champagne glass place a cube of sugar, add Galliano and fill with chilled champagne. Stir to dissolve sugar. Garnish with a strawberry and a sprig of mint.

BLACK FOREST

30 ml (1 fl oz) Kahlua
cold champagne

Pour Kahlua into a highball glass and top up with cold champagne.

BLACK VELVET

¹/₂ champagne (chilled)
¹/₂ stout (chilled)

Pour champagne and stout simultaneously and slowly into a champagne glass and serve.

GISELLE

15 ml (¹/₂ fl oz) blue curaçao
champagne

In a champagne glass, pour curaçao and top up with chilled champagne. Garnish with a twist of lemon and a sprig of mint.

CHAMPAGNE COCKTAIL

cube sugar
Angostura bitters
15 ml (¹/₂ fl oz) brandy
chilled champagne
maraschino cherry

In a champagne glass place a cube of sugar.
Saturate with bitters.
Add brandy.
Fill with chilled champagne.
Stir only to dissolve sugar.
Serve with a
cherry.

APERITIFS

An aperitif is a drink to stimulate one's appetite and is usually a wine based cocktail. The most popular six aperitifs are sherry, vermouth, Dubonnet, Byrrh, Rosso Antico and Campari.

Sherry was first produced in Spain near the town of Jerez. Sherries are wines varying in colour from white to dark brown. The four types are extra dry, dry, medium dry and sweet and are usually served in a 60 ml (2 fl oz) sherry glass. Very dry sherry should be chilled, medium sherries should be slightly chilled and sweet sherry should be opened and left standing at room temperature.

Vermouth is probably the most popular of the aperitifs. It is made using white wine such as muscatel, sauterne, white port or even mild sherry as a base, and added to this are strongly flavoured wines which contain as many as fifty different herbs and spices. One of these herbs is 'Wermuth' which, in German, means wormwood. There are four types of vermouth: dry, sometimes known as French which is clear and dry; sweet, sometimes known as Italian which is red and sweet; bianco,

which is gold in colour and is the sweetest and amaro, which is brown in colour and is very bitter.

Dubonnet is a blend of carefully selected old liqueur wines to which Peruvian bark or quinine is added. It has a rich, slightly sweet flavour with the qualities of a mild liqueur. It can be served in a sherry or cocktail glass chilled, with a slice of lemon, or it can be served as a cocktail.

Byrrh (pronounced to rhyme with 'her') is a French wine, fortified with brandy, and with a quinine flavour. The juice of sweet and dry grapes is mixed and passed over a series of aromatic herbs and Peruvian bark to produce its stimulating taste and aroma.

Campari Bitter Aperitif is one of the world's greatest drinks and is exported all over the world from the firm's headquarters in Milan. Its unique, bitter-sweet taste is obtained by the infusion of aromatic and bitter herbs with the fragrance of

orange peel, and it possesses appetising, and at the same time digestive qualities. The product which gives the distinguishing red colour to Campari is a base vegetable oil. Campari is a spirit-based product, distinct from its competitors which are all wine-based.

It was discovered in the nineteenth-century by Gaspare Campari and his son Davide made it world-famous. Popular drinks now include: Campari with lemonade or 7-up, bitter lemon, tonic water or orange juice. Campari is traditionally served as an aperitif: 1/3 Campari, 2/3 soda. Rosso Antico is born from the harmonious blending of selected wines of mature vintage fused with a choice variety of aromatic herbs that give it the delicate aroma and flavour. It is served over ice with a slice of lemon or orange peel, or as a long drink, by adding soda water with a little gin or vodka which accentuates its delicate fragrance.

Rosso Antico extra dry is also a wine-based aperitif containing the choicest red wines aged and blended with the infusion of aromatic and bitter herbs. It mixes well with gin or vodka and orange juice. It is preferred by most just 'on the rocks'.

BLACK POWER

60 ml (2 fl oz) marsala (dessert wine)
cola
3 cubes ice
slice lemon

Top marsala with cola over ice cubes in an old-fashioned glass.
Add a slice of lemon and serve.

MANHATTAN COCKTAIL

23 ml (3/4 fl oz) sweet vermouth
45 ml (1 1/2 fl oz) bourbon or Canadian whisky
dash Angostura bitters (optional)
ice
maraschino cherry

Stir vermouth, whisky and bitters with ice.
Strain into a cocktail glass.
Garnish with a cherry and serve.

GOLDFINGER

8 ml (¹/₄ fl oz) lemon juice
30 ml (1 fl oz) orange juice
60 ml (2 fl oz) Rosso Antico
30 ml (1 fl oz) vodka
ice
twist of lemon
slice of orange

Stir with ice and pour into a champagne glass. Garnish with a twist of lemon and a slice of orange.

AMERICANO COCKTAIL

¹/₂ Campari
¹/₂ sweet vermouth
soda water
slice of lemon

Pour Campari and vermouth over ice and top up with soda water and a slice of lemon.

DUBONNET COCKTAIL

¹/₂ Dubonnet
¹/₂ gin
twist of lemon
ice

Stir Dubonnet and gin with ice.
Strain into a cocktail glass.
Garnish with a twist of lemon and serve.

LIQUEURS AND CORDIALS

The words liqueurs and cordials are synonymous. They describe liquor made by mixing or redistilling neutral spirits with fruits, flowers, herbs, roots, plants, dairy products and juices as well as various beans and nuts. These are the living ingredients which will give life, colour, aroma and flavour to the liqueurs. Liqueurs or cordials are made in all countries and they are closely guarded secret recipes.

Creating liqueurs, for the liqueurist, is a work of art. It was the alchemists who first used alcohol or spirits to explore the process of creating a liqueur. Classic liqueurs can be traced back in history as far as 1510. D.O.M. Benedictine Liqueur is a classic example. It was named by Dom Bernardo Vincelli at the Benedictine Monastery in Fecamp in 1510 and is based on brandy and flavoured with herbs, spices and fruit peel. It was designed to fortify the weary monks. The initials D.O.M. stand for 'Deo Optimo Maximo' – 'To God, most good, most great'.

68

GALLIANO

A smooth gold-coloured liqueur with licorice and anisette flavour.
It may be served straight or with spirits, mixers or juice.

FREDDIE FUDPUKER

ice cubes
30 ml (1 fl oz) tequila
orange juice
15 ml (¹/₂ fl oz) Galliano
cherry

Fill a tall glass with ice cubes. Add tequila and orange juice to fill three-quarters of the glass. Float Galliano on top and garnish with a cherry.

GALLIANO ICE

cracked ice
30 ml (1 fl oz) Galliano
juice of ¹/₄ lime

Fill an old-fashioned glass with ice. Pour Galliano over ice and then squeeze juice into the glass. Stir and serve.

GOLDEN CADILLAC

crushed ice
60 ml (2 fl oz) Galliano
30 ml (1 fl oz) white crème de cacao
30 ml (1 fl oz) cream

Place crushed ice in a cocktail shaker or blender. Shake and strain ingredients into a champagne glass. (A scoop of vanilla ice cream can be substituted for cream.)

GOLDEN TORPEDO

ice
30 ml (1 fl oz) Galliano
15 ml (¹/₂ fl oz) Amaretto di Galliano
30 ml (1 fl oz) cream or ice cream

Place ice in a cocktail shaker or blender. Shake and strain ingredients into a champagne glass. This is a prize-winning recipe.

E.T. RAY OF SUNSHINE

30 ml (1 fl oz) Galliano
champagne

Pour Galliano into a champagne glass and top up with chilled champagne.

ITALIAN STINGER

30 ml (1 fl oz) Galliano
38 ml (1¹/₄ fl oz) brandy
ice

Shake ingredients with cracked ice and strain into cocktail glass.

BOSSA NOVA

30 ml (1 fl oz) Galliano
30 ml (1 fl oz) rum
8 ml (¼ fl oz) apricot brandy
60 ml (2 fl oz) pineapple juice
½ egg white
8 ml (¼ fl oz) lemon juice
slice of orange
pineapple
cherry

Shake ingredients in a blender or cocktail shaker. Serve in a tall glass with ice and garnish with a slice of orange, a cherry and a stick or ring of pineapple.

GOLDEN DREAM

30 ml (1 fl oz) Galliano
15 ml (½ fl oz) Cointreau
15 ml (½ fl oz) orange juice
15 ml (½ fl oz) cream
ice

Shake or blend ingredients with ice and strain into a champagne glass.
This is a prize-winning recipe from the United Kingdom Bartenders' Guild.

HARVEY WALLBANGER

ice
180 ml (6 fl oz) orange juice
30 ml (1 fl oz) vodka
splash of Galliano
slice of orange
cherry

In a highball glass with ice pour vodka and orange juice and stir. Splash Galliano on top. Garnish with a slice of orange and a cherry.

TIA MARIA

A Jamaican liqueur
with a rum base and coffee flavour.

TIA MARIA KISS

30 ml (1 fl oz) Tia Maria
fresh cream
cherry

In a liqueur glass pour the Tia Maria and top up
with fresh cream. Add a cherry on two toothpicks
on the rim of the glass.

TIA & COLA

30 ml (1 fl oz) Tia Maria
cola
ice

In a tall glass pour Tia Maria and top up with cola
and ice.

OPERA HOUSE

30 ml (1 fl oz) Tia Maria
15 ml (1/2 fl oz) Cointreau
30 ml (1 fl oz) Cream
30 ml (1 fl oz) brandy

Shake with ice and strain into a champagne glass.

BROWN COW

30 ml (1 fl oz) Tia Maria
milk
ice

In a tall glass pour Tia Maria and top up with milk
and ice.

SWEET MARIA

30 ml (1 fl oz) Tia Maria
30 ml (1 fl oz) bourbon
30 ml (1 fl oz) cream or 1 scoop of ice cream
1 strawberry
nutmeg

Shake or blend ingredients with ice and strain into a champagne glass.
Garnish with a strawberry and dust with nutmeg.

LOVER'S COCKTAIL

60 ml (2 fl oz) Tia Maria
30 ml (1 fl oz) Tequila
ice
maraschino cherry

Stir with ice and strain into a cocktail glass. Garnish with a cherry.

BLACK ROOTS

ice
30 ml (1 fl oz) advokaat liqueur
lemonade or 7-up
30 ml (1 fl oz) Tia Maria

In a highball glass pour the advokaat and then fill the glass with lemonade until it is three-quarters full. Float the Tia Maria on top.

MIDORI MELON LIQUEUR

A Japanese liqueur
with a light fresh taste of honeydew.

MIDORI STRAIGHT

Pour Midori into a liqueur glass.

MIDORI

'with your favourite'

60 ml (2 fl oz) Midori

Top up with soda water, tonic water, dry ginger ale, 7-up or lemonade.
Serve with ice and a straw in a tall glass.

MIDORI ALEXANDER

60 ml (2 fl oz) Midori
30 ml (1 fl oz) brandy or gin
60 ml (2 fl oz) cream or 2 scoops ice cream
ice

Blend or shake ingredients with ice.
Strain into a champagne glass and garnish with mint and a slice of lemon.

SAYONARA COCKTAIL

30 ml (1 fl oz) Midori melon liqueur
30 ml (1 fl oz) blue curaçao
30 ml (1 fl oz) Suntory vodka
dash of egg white
ice

Shake with ice and strain into a highball glass.

GREEN FANTASY

30 ml (1 fl oz) Suntory vodka
30 ml (1 fl oz) dry vermouth
30 ml (1 fl oz) Midori melon liqueur
8 ml (1/4 fl oz) lime juice
ice

Stir in a mixing glass with ice and strain into a cocktail glass. Australian Cocktail from 1982 Championships.

GEISHA LADY

30 ml (1 fl oz) Midori melon liqueur
15 ml (1/2 fl oz) crème de banana
30 ml (1 fl oz) light rum
30 ml (1 fl oz) cream
dash of grenadine
ice

Shake with ice and strain into a champagne glass.

MELON BALL SOUR

15 ml (1/2 fl oz) lemon or lime juice
60 ml (1/2 fl oz) Midori
1 teaspoon egg white
30 ml (1 fl oz) Vodka
scoop of honeydew melon

Blend or shake ingredients with ice in a shaker.
Strain into a sour glass.
Garnish with a scoop of melon and a cherry.

MIDORI COOLER

60 ml (2 fl oz) Midori
ice
soda water
twist of lemon
mint

In a tall glass, pour Midori over ice. Top with soda water and garnish with a twist of lemon and mint.

MIDORI OLD-FASHIONED

dash Angostura bitters
60 ml (2 fl oz) Midori
30 ml (1 fl oz) bourbon
club soda
1/2 slice orange, 1 cherry and twist of lemon

Take an old-fashioned glass and add a dash of Angostura bitters then ice. Add Midori and bourbon. Top up with soda.
Garnish with 1/2 slice of orange and a cherry on a toothpick on the side of the glass. Put a twist of lemon in the glass and serve with a swizzle stick or straw.

COINTREAU

A sweet colourless liqueur
with an orange flavour.

CARIBBEAN COCKTAIL

30 ml (1 fl oz) Cointreau
15 ml (1/2 fl oz) orange curaçao
30 ml (1 fl oz) brandy
ice
twist of orange

Stir with ice in a mixing glass. Strain into a cocktail glass and garnish with a twist of orange.

OPAL COCKTAIL

30 ml (1 fl oz) Cointreau
8 ml (1/4 fl oz) Pernod
8 ml (1/4 fl oz) Galliano
8 ml (1/4 fl oz) blue curaçao
15 ml (1/2 fl oz) vodka
ice

Stir with ice in a mixing glass and strain into a cocktail glass.

TOP OF THE SHEETS

30 ml (1 fl oz) Cointreau
30 ml (1 fl oz) Bacardi rum
30 ml (1 fl oz) brandy
dash lemon juice
dash of egg white
ice
2 maraschino cherries

Shake with ice and strain into a cocktail glass. Garnish with cherries.

COINTREAU AND COFFEE BEANS

30 ml (1 fl oz) Cointreau
2 coffee beans

Pour Cointreau and coffee beans into a liqueur glass and light with a match. Allow to cool and sip with your favourite coffee.

FOXI COCKTAIL

30 ml (1 fl oz) Cointreau
30 ml (1 fl oz) dark rum
60 ml (2 fl oz) pineapple juice
ice

Blend with ice and strain into a champagne glass.

TIGHT LIPS

30 ml (1 fl oz) Cointreau
15 ml (1/2 fl oz) Grenadine
30 ml (1 fl oz) Bacardi rum
dash of egg white
ice

Shake with ice and strain into a cocktail glass.

HOT DREAM

30 ml (1 fl oz) Cointreau
15 ml (1/2 fl oz) Galliano
30 ml (1 fl oz) pineapple juice
30 ml (1 fl oz) cream
ice

Shake with ice and strain into a champagne glass.

COINTREAU SUN RISER

ice
30 ml (1 fl oz) Cointreau
60 ml (2 fl oz) orange juice
1 teaspoon grenadine
twist of lemon
cherry

Fill an old-fashioned glass with ice.
Pour in Cointreau and orange juice, then 1 teaspoon grenadine. Do not stir.
Garnish with a twist of lemon and cherry.

NAPOLEON COCKTAIL

30 ml (1 fl oz) Cointreau
30 ml (1 fl oz) brandy
30 ml (1 fl oz) pineapple juice
dash of grenadine
piece of pineapple
slice of orange
cherry

Shake or blend ingredients with ice and strain into a champagne glass.
Garnish with a piece of pineapple, a slice of orange and a cherry.

COINTREAU OLD FASHIONED WAY

30 ml (1 fl oz) brandy
cube of sugar
2 dashes Angostura bitters
30 ml (1 fl oz) Cointreau

Place brandy in an old-fashioned glass with ice.
Add sugar and Angostura bitters, then float Cointreau on top.
Garnish with a sprig of mint, a slice of orange and a strawberry.

BAILEYS IRISH CREAM LIQUEUR

The Gaelic word for cream is 'Uachtar' which, according to Celtic legend, literally means 'Irish cream is as natural and wholesome as ever'. Fine old whiskey provides the base for Baileys original Irish Cream. The alcohol content of Baileys acts as a natural preservative for the cream.

BAILEYS IRISH CREAM AND MILK

60 ml (2 fl oz) Baileys Irish Cream
milk
ice

Top up with milk and add ice if desired.

BAILEYS IRISH COFFEE

Follow the recipe for Irish Coffee, substituting Baileys Irish Cream for Irish Whiskey.

BAILEYS IRISH CREAM STRAIGHT

60 ml (2 fl oz) Baileys Irish Cream in a sherry glass.

BILL BAILEY

60 ml (2 fl oz) Bailey's Irish Cream
30 ml (1 fl oz) vodka
soda water
ice

Pour over ice in a highball glass and top up with soda.

CARESSER

30 ml (1 fl oz) Bailey's Irish Cream
30 ml (1 fl oz) Bacardi rum
ice
milk

Pour ingredients into a highball glass with ice and top up with milk.

TEMPTATION

30 ml (1 fl oz) Bailey's Irish Cream
30 ml (1 fl oz) gin
ice

Stir with ice and strain into a champagne glass.

SPANISH JOE

30 ml (1 fl oz) Bailey's Irish Cream
30 ml (1 fl oz) tequila
ice

Serve in an old-fashioned glass over ice.

WEDDING COCKTAIL

60 ml (2 fl oz) Baileys Irish Cream
30 ml (1 fl oz) Bacardi or light rum

Stir in a mixing
glass with ice
and serve in a
champagne
glass.

PADDY O'HOOLIGAN

60 ml (2 fl oz) Baileys Irish Cream
30 ml (1 fl oz) green crème de menthe
sprig of mint

Place ingredients in an old-fashioned glass, with
ice, and stir.
Garnish with a sprig of mint.

MOTHER MCCREE

60 ml (2 fl oz) Baileys Irish Cream
30 ml (1 fl oz) coconut milk
30 ml (1 fl oz) vodka
dash of grenadine

Shake or blend with ice, then strain into a champagne glass.

GRAND MARNIER

It was Louis Alexandre Marnier-Lapostolle who finally ended the family quest for the perfect liqueur. He discovered that the blend of wild bitter oranges with the finest cognac could produce a liqueur of distinction. His countless experiments eventually led him to blend the exotic oranges with his prized cognacs from the Charente region in France – and so Grand Marnier was born.

TOP DOG

30 ml (1 fl oz) Grand Marnier
30 ml (1 fl oz) gin
15 ml (¹/₂ fl oz) sweet vermouth
ice

Stir with ice in a mixing glass and strain into a cocktail glass.

NOBLE COCKTAIL

30 ml (1 fl oz) Grand Marnier
60 ml (2 fl oz) orange juice
30 ml (1 fl oz) cognac brandy
ice

Stir with ice in mixing glass and strain into a cocktail glass.

HAITI COCKTAIL

30 ml (1 fl oz) Grand Marnier
30 ml (1 fl oz) brandy
white wine
ice
slice of lemon
slice of orange
sprig of mint
maraschino cherry

Pour ingredients into a highball glass with ice and top up with white wine. Garnish with lemon, orange, mint and a cherry.

SWINGER COCKTAIL

30 ml (1 fl oz) Grand Marnier
30 ml (1 fl oz) vodka
30 ml (1 fl oz) Cinzano sweet vermouth
ice

Stir with ice in a mixing glass and strain into a cocktail glass.

GRAND MARNIER SNIFTER

60 ml (2 fl oz) Grand Marnier
twist of orange

Serve in a brandy balloon glass. Garnish with a twist of orange.

GRAND MARNIER AND CHAMPAGNE

30 ml (1 fl oz) Grand Marnier
chilled champagne
slice of orange
strawberry

Place ingredients in a champagne glass and garnish with a slice of orange and a strawberry.

GRAND MARNIER STRAIGHT

Pour into a liqueur glass.

RED LION

30 ml (1 fl oz) Grand Marnier
30 ml (1 fl oz) gin
60 ml (2 fl oz) orange juice
15 ml (½ fl oz) lemon juice
ice
twist of lemon

Shake or blend ingredients with ice and serve in a wine goblet.
Garnish with a twist of orange.

ALFONSO COCKTAIL

15 ml (½ fl oz) gin
15 ml (½ fl oz) dry vermouth
30 ml (1 fl oz) Grand Marnier
15 ml (½ fl oz) Sweet vermouth
dash Angostura bitters

Shake or blend ingredients with ice and strain into a champagne glass.

AFTER DAWN

60 ml (2 fl oz) Grand Marnier
coffee
sugar to taste
whipped cream

Into a coffee cup pour sugar and Grand Marnier, then add hot coffee and top with whipped cream.

SOUTHERN COMFORT

This liqueur was born in New Orleans when one gentleman wasn't entirely happy with the taste of the finest whiskies so he combined rare and delicious ingredients to create a superb, unusually smooth, special kind of basic liquor. Its formula is still a family secret.

SLOE'N COMFORT ABLE

ice
30 ml (1 fl oz) Southern Comfort
orange juice

In a highball glass put ice and Southern Comfort. Top up with orange juice and garnish with slice of orange.

HOT BUTTERED COMFORT

small stick cinnamon
slice of lemon peel
45 ml (1 1/2 fl oz) Southern Comfort
pat of butter

Put a spoon in a mug and place lemon peel, cinnamon and Southern Comfort in the mug. Top up with boiling water, then float butter on top and stir.

COMFORT "OLD-FASHIONED"

dash Angostura bitters
1/2 teaspoon sugar (optional)
15 ml (1/2 fl oz) soda water
45 ml (1 1/2 fl oz) Southern Comfort
twist of lemon
twist of orange
cherry

Pour bitters, sugar and soda water in an old-fashioned glass and stir.
Add ice cubes and Southern Comfort. Garnish with a twist of lemon, a twist of orange peel and a cherry.

THE AMERICA'S CUP

30 ml (1 fl oz) Southern Comfort
15 ml (1/2 fl oz) Bacardi rum
15 ml (1/2 fl oz) Galliano
30 ml (1 fl oz) pineapple juice
30 ml (1 fl oz) orange juice
60 ml (2 fl oz) cream
ice
pineapple wedge
sprig of mint

Shake with ice and strain into a silver mug or a 6 oz glass. Garnish with pineapple and mint.

BIRTHDAY COCKTAIL

30 ml (1 fl oz) Southern Comfort
60 ml (2 fl oz) cream
15 ml (1/2 fl oz) crème de cacao
ice

Shake with ice and strain into a cocktail glass.

MEMPHIS BELLE

half a peach
maraschino cherry
shaved ice
Southern Comfort

Place half a peach and a maraschino cherry in a champagne glass. Add shaved ice and fill with Southern Comfort. Serve with short straws and a small spoon.

SICILIAN KISS

60 ml (2 fl oz) Southern Comfort
30 ml (1 fl oz) Amaretto
ice
1 green and 1 red cherry

Pour ingredients into a glass with ice and stir. Garnish with cherries.

SOUTHERN LOVE

30 ml (1 fl oz) brandy
30 ml (1 fl oz) Southern Comfort
30 ml (1 fl oz) cream
ice
mint
strawberry

Shake and strain ingredients with ice into a champagne glass. Garnish with mint and strawberry.

DRAMBUIE

A liqueur from Scotland based on Scotch Whisky and Heather Honey.

WILD STRAWBERRIES

4 strawberries
60 ml (2 fl oz) Drambuie
1 scoop whipped cream
nutmeg

Wash and hull strawberries, sprinkle with sugar, add Drambuie then refrigerate until chilled. Serve in champagne glass and add whipped cream then sprinkle nutmeg on top.

JUMPING JACK

30 ml (1 fl oz) Drambuie
30 ml (1 fl oz) vodka
15 ml (1/2 fl oz) Galliano
8 ml (1/4 fl oz) lemon or lime juice
dash egg white
ice
maraschino cherry

Shake with ice and serve strained in a cocktail glass. Garnish with a cherry.

JUNGLE JUICE

30 ml (1 fl oz) Drambuie
30 ml (1 fl oz) Bacardi rum
30 ml (1 fl oz) coconut milk
30 ml (1 fl oz) cream
30 ml (1 fl oz) pineapple juice
1/2 a banana
ice

Blend with ice and banana. Serve in a highball glass.

DRAMBUIE SRAIGHT

Serve in a liqueur glass.

DRAMBUIE SNIFTER

60 ml (2 fl oz) Drambuie
30 ml (1 fl oz) brandy

Serve in a brandy balloon glass.

DRAMBUIE SOUR

Follow the recipe for Tennessee Sour (page 25), substituting Drambuie for whisky.

DRAMBUIE AND YOUR FAVOURITE

Popular mixers include: soda, dry ginger ale, 7-up or lemonade and fruit juice. Just add ice and serve.

PRINCE CHARLES

45 ml (1¹/₂ fl oz) Drambuie
45 ml (1¹/₂ fl oz) brandy
ice
cherry

In an old-fashioned glass, with ice, add the Drambuie and brandy.
Garnish with a cherry.

DRAMBUIE COCKTAIL

45 ml (1¹/₂ fl oz) Drambuie
45 ml (1¹/₂ fl oz) sweet vermouth
cherry

Stir in a mixing glass with ice.
Strain into a cocktail glass.
Garnish with
a cherry.

RUSTY NAIL

30 ml (1 fl oz) Drambuie
45 ml (1¹/₂ fl oz) Scotch whisky

Serve with ice in an old-fashioned glass.

BENEDICTINE (D.O.M.)

This liqueur is supposed to have originated in the sixteenth century in a Benedictine monastery. It is a herb-flavoured liqueur with a brandy base.

B AND B

1 part Benedictine
1 part cognac or brandy

Serve in a liqueur glass.

BENEDICTINE STRAIGHT

30 ml (1 fl oz) Benedictine

Serve in a liqueur glass.

SUNDOWNER

30 ml (1 fl oz) Benedictine
30 ml (1 fl oz) dark rum
60 ml (2 fl oz) orange juice
ice
slice of orange
maraschino cherry

Rim a champagne glass with caster (powdered) sugar. Shake with ice and strain into glass. Garnish with slice of orange and cherry.

DOM

60 ml (2 fl oz) Benedictine
soda water
slice of lemon

Place Benedictine with ice in a highball glass and top up with club soda. Garnish with a slice of lemon.

MOONGLOW

60 ml (2 fl oz) Benedictine
30 ml (1 fl oz) crème de cacao
60 ml (2 fl oz) cream
ice

Shake with ice and serve in a 180 ml (6 fl oz) globlet.

E.T. AND D.O.M.

30 ml (1 fl oz) D.O.M. Benedictine
60 ml (2 fl oz) banana pineapple nectar
60 ml (2 fl oz) cream or a scoop of ice cream
60 ml (2 fl oz) blue curaçao
slice of banana
mint
2 cherries
strawberry

Shake ingredients in a blender or cocktail shaker. Serve in a brandy balloon or snifter glass and garnish with the banana slice, mint, cherries and strawberry on a toothpick.

CAFÉ BENEDICTINE

60 ml (2 fl oz) Benedictine
hot black coffee
cream

In a coffee cup add Benectine and pour hot coffee. Using the back of a teaspoon float cream on the top. Do not stir.

BENEDICTINE COCKTAIL

30 ml (1 fl oz) Benedictine
15 ml (1/2 fl oz) dry vermouth
15 ml (1/2 fl oz) whisky

Stir in a mixing glass with ice and serve in a cocktail glass.

ASSORTED DRINKS

ASSORTED DRINKS

Collins; Coolers; Crustas; Daisies; Egg Noggs; Fixes; Fizzes; Flips; Frappés; Gimlet; Highball; Old-fashioned; Rickeys; Slings; Smashes; Scaffas; Sours; Toddies.

Collins

These are long drinks which should be served in a highball glass and there are recipes by the dozen. Before 1939 a 'John Collins' was made with Dutch gin and 'Tom Collins' with 'Old Tom' gin. Nowadays Tom Collins is made with dry gin. John Collins is made with Dutch gin.

Coolers

These 'cousins' to the Collins drinks are also summer or hot weather drinks, as they are long and refreshing and made with plenty of ice.

RUM COOLER

60 ml (2 fl oz) lemon juice
4 dashes grenadine
60 ml (2 fl oz) rum
fruit for garnish

Shake lemon juice, grenadine and rum with ice. Strain into a highball glass. Add cracked ice. Fill with soda water. Garnish with fruit.

GIN COOLER

cracked ice
1/2 tablespoon sugar
60 ml (2 fl oz) lemon juice
60 ml (2 fl oz) gin
ginger beer
fruit for garnish

Place ice in a glass. Add sugar, lemon juice and gin. Fill with ginger beer. Garnish with fruit.

Crustas

To be served in a champagne glass.
Firstly rub the rim of the glass with a slice of lemon and dip into a plate containing caster (powdered) sugar.

BRANDY CRUSTA

dash Angostura bitters
90 ml (3 fl oz) brandy
3 dashes maraschino
maraschino cherry

Shake bitters, brandy and maraschino. Strain into a champagne glass. Add a cherry and serve.
Note: Gin, rum or whisky can be substituted for brandy. In Australia it is common to add 1 teaspoon lemon juice and 2 teaspoons orange juice to this recipe.

Daisies

These are pleasant, iced drinks lavishly decorated with fresh fruit and refreshing for summer. 'They are served in 180 ml (6 fl oz) goblet.'

BRANDY DAISY

60 ml (2 fl oz) brandy
30 ml (1 fl oz) lemon juice
6 dashes grenadine
fruit and mint for garnish

Fill a goblet with cracked ice. Shake brandy, lemon juice and grenadine. Strain and add soda water. Garnish with fruit and sprigs of mint and serve.

Egg Noggs

Egg noggs are delicious served warm or cold. They are very rich so, if you are preparing them for several people, it is wiser to make small amounts as one or two glasses go a long way.

EGGSOTIC

45 ml (1 1/2 fl oz) dry gin
1 teaspoon caster (powdered) sugar
juice of 1/2 lemon
90 ml (3 fl oz) champagne
1 egg
twist of lemon

Combine gin, sugar and lemon juice and shake with ice, together with egg. Strain into a highball glass. Fill with champagne, add a twist of lemon and serve. It is important that you do not stir this cocktail – the champagne will lose its effervescence.

EGG ROYAL COCKTAIL

30 ml (1 fl oz) brandy
30 ml (1 fl oz) port wine
dash white curaçao
1 egg yolk
1 teaspoon sugar
ice
nutmeg

Shake brandy, port wine, curaçao, egg yolk and sugar with ice. Strain into a cocktail glass and sprinkle nutmeg on top.

DREAM FOR LOVERS

(2 persons)

30 ml (1 fl oz) Galliano
30 ml (1 fl oz) orange juice
15 ml (1/2 fl oz) Cointreau
30 ml (1 fl oz) cream
1 egg

Shake and strain with ice and serve in a champagne glass.

EGG ALEXANDER

30 ml (1 fl oz) brandy
30 ml (1 fl oz) brown crème de cacao
30 ml (1 fl oz) cream
1 egg
ice

Mix with an egg beater or electric blender with ice. Strain and pour into a champagne glass.

EGG SOUR

60 ml (2 fl oz) bourbon (or Canadian whisky,
Southern Comfort, Southern Mist
or Southern Society)
30 ml (1 fl oz) lemon juice
1 teaspoon sugar
1 egg

Mix ingredients with ice, with an egg beater or electric blender.
Strain and pour into a sour glass. Garnish with a slice of orange and a cherry.

Fixes

These are served in a 180 ml (6 fl oz) glass with shaved ice.

BRANDY FIX

30 ml (1 fl oz) brandy
30 ml (1 fl oz) cherry brandy
1 teaspoon sugar
1 teaspoon water
30 ml (1 fl oz) lemon juice
slice of lemon

Stir brandy, cherry brandy, sugar, water and lemon juice.
Add slice of lemon and serve.
Note: Rum, gin and whisky fixes are made as above but minus brandy and cherry brandy.

Fizzes

Another drink similar to those in the Collins family. It is usually served in a 210 ml (7 fl oz) glass.

RAMOZ FIZZ

60 ml (2 fl oz) dry gin
30 ml (2 fl oz) lemon juice
30 ml (2 fl oz) lime juice
30 ml (2 fl oz) heavy cream
2 dashes orange flower water
1 egg white
1 teaspoon sugar
cracked ice

Shake ingredients vigorously and thoroughly with cracked ice.
Strain into a highball glass with its edge frosted with lemon and sugar, and serve.

NEW ORLEANS FIZZ

60 ml (2 fl oz) dry gin
30 ml (1 fl oz) lemon juice
1 rounded teaspoon sugar
30 ml (1 fl oz) sweet cream
white of 1 egg
2 or 3 dashes orange flower water
dash vanilla
cracked ice
soda water

Shake ingredients with cracked ice until thoroughly mixed and frothy.
Strain into a highball glass. Fill with soda water and serve.

BACARDI FIZZ

60 ml (2 fl oz) Bacardi rum
1 teaspoon sugar
60 ml (2 fl oz) lemon juice
ice
soda water

Shake rum, sugar and lemon juice well with ice and strain.
Fill with soda water and serve.
Note: Gin, any whisky, or brandy can be used instead of rum.
Golden Fizz is a spirit fizz to which the yolk of an egg has been added.
Silver Fizz is a spirit fizz to which the white of an egg has been added.

EGG NOGG

1 egg
1 tablespoon sugar
30 ml (1 fl oz) brandy
milk
nutmeg

Shake egg, sugar and brandy well.
Strain into a highball glass or goblet.
Fill with milk.
Sprinkle nutmeg on top and
serve. Note: Gin, rum or
whisky can be
subsituted for
brandy.

GRASSHOPPER

30 ml (1 fl oz) white crème de cacao
45 ml (1 1/2 fl oz) green crème de menthe
60 ml (2 fl oz) fresh cream
cracked ice

Shake crème de cacao, crème de menthe and
cream with ice.
Strain into a champagne glass and serve.

TOM COLLINS

cracked ice
60 ml (2 fl oz) lemon juice
1 teaspoon sugar
60 ml (2 fl oz) dry gin
soda water
slice lemon
maraschino cherry

Put cracked ice, lemon juice,
sugar and gin in a glass. Fill
with soda water and stir.
Serve with a slice of lemon
and cherry for garnish.
Note: Brandy, bourbon, rum
or any whisky can be
used instead of gin.

FLUFFY DUCK No 1

30 ml (1 fl oz) advokaat
15 ml (1/2 fl oz) orange curaçao
15 ml (1/2 fl oz) cream
cherry
slice of orange

Serve in a highball glass with ice. Top up with lemonade then garnish with a cherry and a slice of orange.

PUERTO RICO RICKEY

Follow the recipe given for Gin Rickey and then add 2 dashes of raspberry syrup.

PIMM'S

3 cubes ice
45 ml (1 1/2 fl oz) Pimm's No 1
ginger ale (or lemonade)
slice cucumber
slice orange
maraschino cherry

In a highball glass place the ice cubes. Add Pimm's. Top with ginger ale. Garnish with a slice of cucumber, a slice of orange and a cherry.

Flips

The Flip, particularly the variety made with rum, is renowned as an old-fashioned drink. It once was very popular among sailors. It should be served in a 180 ml (6 fl oz) goblet.

BRANDY FLIP

60 ml (2 fl oz) brandy
1 teaspoon sugar
1 whole egg
ice
nutmeg

Shake brandy, sugar and egg with ice.
Strain.
Sprinkle nutmeg on top and serve.
Note: Rum, whisky, claret, port, sherry or blackberry brandy can be used instead of brandy.

Frappés

Frappés can be made from any liquor or liqueur or combination of both.
The simplest method is to fill a 150 ml (5 fl oz) glass with shaved ice and pour 30 ml (1 fl oz) of the liqueur you desire over it. Serve with a drinking straw.

Gimlet

This drink has a very interesting history. It started its life on the sailing ships of old which travelled the Atlantic. Due to lack of vitamins in the diet of the sailors on board these ships, the crew very often suffered from scurvy. To counteract this, they were issued with fresh limes high in vitamin C which were able to be stored. To encourage the sailors to eat this fruit, they were issued with a tot of gin to mix with the juice of the lime and so the 'Gimlet' was born.

GIMLET COCKTAIL

²/₃ dry gin
¹/₃ Roses lime juice
twist of lemon

In a mixing glass put ice, add gin and lime juice. Stir. Strain into a cocktail glass. Serve with a twist of lemon.

Highball

The story of the 'Highball' goes back to the days when the railways were being constructed in the United States. As each section of the railway was completed, a signal was raised, usually a telegraph pole with a large white disc on it. When the men saw the 'Highball' raised they knew that it was time for a rest period which consisted of a long cool drink which was not strong, but stimulating and thirst quenching.

BOURBON HIGHBALL

ice
2 dashes bitters
60 ml (2 fl oz) bourbon
soda water or dry ginger ale
twist of lemon

Place ice in a highball glass.
Add bitters and bourbon.
Fill with soda water or dry ginger ale. Garnish with a twist of lemon and serve.

Rickeys

These long drinks keep to a spirit for their base, to which both the juice and rind of a lime or lemon are added. The glass is filled with iced soda water or other charged water.
Serve in a 180 ml (6 fl oz) glass.

GIN RICKEY

60 ml (2 fl oz) gin
30 ml (1 fl oz) lime juice
ice
soda water
twist of lemon

Pour gin and lime juice into a glass over ice.
Top with soda water.
Serve with the rind of a lemon placed in the glass.
Note: Applejack, bourbon, rum or any whisky can be substituted for gin.

HUGO RICKEY

Follow the recipe given for Gin Rickey and then add 2 dashes of grenadine. Garnish with a slice of pineapple.

Slings

Properly made, the contemporary Sling should consist of a brandy, whisky or gin base. Sugar and nutmeg may be added, according to the other ingredients used. Use a highball glass filled with ice.

GIN SLING

ice
60 ml (2 fl oz) gin
30 ml (1 fl oz) lemon juice
dash grenadine
soda water or water
slice of lemon
maraschino cherry

Pour gin, lemon juice and grenadine into a glass. Top with soda water or water.
Garnish with a slice of lemon and a cherry and serve.
Note: Brandy, rum and whisky can be used instead of gin.

GOLD COAST PARADISE

This is a prize winning cocktail,
created by Ian Orton

30 ml (1 fl oz) vodka
15 ml (1/2 fl oz) Galliano
15 ml (1/2 fl oz) rockmelon pulp
dash lemon juice
ice
strawberry

Put the vodka, galliano, rockmelon and lemon
juice into a blender with ice and strain into a
cocktail glass. Garnish with a strawberry on the
side of the glass.

BRANDY SMASH

1 teaspoon sugar
water
2 sprigs mint
cracked ice
60 ml (2 fl oz) brandy

Dissolve sugar with a little water and sprigs of
mint.
Muddle this and add cracked ice.
Pour brandy over the ice.
Garnish with mint and serve with drinking straws.
Note: Gin, rum or any whisky can be used instead
of brandy.

SANGAREE

This is an Old-Fashioned without the bitters
and which always includes nutmeg. It can be
made with gin, whisky, rum or sherry
instead of brandy.

1/2 teaspoon sugar
water
30 ml (1 fl oz) brandy
ice
nutmeg

In an old-fashioned glass, put a half teaspoon of
sugar dissolved in a little water. Then add brandy
and ice. Stir and serve with a sprinkling of nutmeg.

Sours

Serve in a 180 ml (6 fl oz) glass.

WHISKY SOUR

These are served in an old-fashioned glass.

60 ml (2 fl oz) Canadian whisky
30 ml (1 fl oz) lemon juice
1/2 teaspoon sugar
few drops egg white
soda water
slice orange
maraschino cherry

Shake whisky, lemon juice, sugar and egg white
and strain. Top with soda water.
Garnish with a slice of orange and a cherry and
serve.
Note: Any whisky, bourbon, or tequila can be
used.

SCAFFA

30 ml (1 fl oz) brandy (or gin or whisky)
dash Angostura bitters
30 ml (1 fl oz) Benedictine

In a cocktail glass (without ice) add the ingredients. Stir and serve.

Toddies

Serve in an old-fashioned glass or mug.

BRANDY TODDY

1 teaspoon sugar
water
ice cubes
60 ml (2 fl oz) brandy

Dissolve sugar with a little water in a glass or mug.
Add ice cubes and brandy.
Stir and serve.
Note: Bacardi, Calvados, gin or whisky can be sub-
stituted for brandy.

HOT TODDIES

These are served in an old-fashioned
glass or mug.

45 ml (1 1/2 fl oz) any spirit
1 teaspoon sugar
2 cloves
slice of lemon
1 stick cinnamon

Mix spirit, sugar, cloves, lemon and cinnamon.
Add boiling water. (If the drink is prepared in a
glass, pour the boiling water over a silver spoon.
This will prevent the glass from cracking.) Serve.

MISCELLANEOUS COCKTAILS

AVALANCHE

15 ml ($1/2$ fl oz) Sambuca di Galliano
30 ml (1 fl oz) white rum
15 ml ($1/2$ fl oz) blue curacao
ice
lemonade

Pour the Sambuca, rum and curacao into a highball glass over ice. Top with lemonade.

ANGEL'S KISS

There are many variations of this after dinner drink but we will leave it up to you to choose your own 'Angel's Kiss'.

23 ml ($3/4$ fl oz) apricot liqueur
8 ml ($1/4$ fl oz) crème de cacao
8 ml ($1/4$ fl oz) crème de violette
8 ml ($1/4$ fl oz) Prunelle
8 ml ($1/4$ fl oz) fresh cream
8 ml ($1/4$ fl oz) thick cream

These ingredients are poured carefully into a pousse café glass in the order given so the different liqueurs do not mix.

1/6 maraschino liqueur
1/6 Parfait Amour
1/6 yellow chartreuse
1/6 Benedictine
1/6 cognac
1/6 fresh cream

These ingredients are poured carefully into a pousse café glass in the order given so the different liqueurs do not mix.

ANGEL'S LIPS

20 ml ($2/3$ fl oz) Benedictine
10 ml ($1/3$ fl oz) fresh cream

In a liqueur glass pour Benedictine and float the cream on top.

BULLSHOT

1 cube beef stock
60 ml (2 fl oz) hot water
$1/4$ tablespoon celery salt or salt
fresh lemon
30-38 ml (1-1 $1/4$ fl oz) vodka
ice
lemon peel

Dissolve a stock cube in hot water.
Add celery salt or salt, a squeeze of fresh lemon and vodka.
Stir vigorously.
Serve on the rocks in an old-fashioned glass with lemon peel garnish.
Note: Rum can be substituted for vodka.

CAFE ROYALE

1 lump sugar
demi-tasse cup of hot black coffee
1 teaspoon brandy

Place sugar in a teaspoon and balance over a demi-tasse cup of hot coffee.
Fill the spoon with brandy and, when it is warm, blaze with a lighted match.
As the flame begins to fade, put the spoon into the coffee, and then serve.

EGG SOUR

1 tablespoon caster (powdered) sugar
juice of $1/4$ lemon
30 ml (1 fl oz) white curaçao
30 ml (1 fl oz) brandy
1 whole egg
cracked ice

Shake caster sugar, lemon juice, curaçao, brandy and egg with cracked ice.
Strain into a sour glass and serve.

NEGRONI

30 ml (1 fl oz) dry gin
15 ml ($1/2$ fl oz) Campari bitters
23 ml ($3/4$ fl oz) sweet vermouth
ice
soda water
lemon peel

Stir gin, bitters and vermouth in a mixing glass with ice. Pour into a 150-180 ml (5 fl oz) glass.
Add a splash of soda water and lemon peel and serve.

FLUFFY DUCK No 2

60 ml (2 fl oz) advokaat
orange juice
ice
slice of orange

Pour advokaat into a highball glass with ice and top up with orange juice.
Garnish with a slice of orange.

Pousse Café

(original recipe)

5 ml (1/6 fl oz) grenadine
5 ml (1/6 fl oz) crème de cacao dark liqueur
5 ml (1/6 fl oz) maraschino liqueur
5 ml (1/6 fl oz) green crème de menthe liqueur
5 ml (1/6 fl oz) crème Yvette liqueur
5 ml (1/6 fl oz) brandy

Pour the liqueurs into a 30 ml (1 fl oz) liqueur glass over the back of a spoon, held so that it touches the edge of the inside of the glass. The pouring must be done very carefully to prevent the liqueurs mixing and requires a certain amount of patience.
Note: Pour the ingredients in the order given in the recipe as liqueurs differ in weight.

Zazerac

1 cube sugar
dash Angostura bitters
dash soda water
3 ice cubes
30 ml (1 fl oz) bourbon or rye
1/2 teaspoon Pernod or Ricard
slice of orange
maraschino cherry
lemon peel

Put a cube of sugar in an old-fashioned glass.
Add Angostura bitters.
Dissolve sugar with bitters and soda water.
Add ice and bourbon or rye.
Float Pernod or Ricard on top.
Garnish with a slice of orange on one side and a cherry on the other side.
Put the lemon peel in the glass and serve with a swizzle stick.

Lady Lynne

45 ml (1 1/2 fl oz) gin
30 ml (1 fl oz) Parfait Amour
8 ml (1/4 fl oz) lime or lemon juice
dash of egg white
ice
strawberry

Shake with ice and serve in a cocktail glass. Garnish with a strawberry.

K.J. Sledge Hammer

30 ml (1 fl oz) Kahlua
30 ml (1 fl oz) vodka
cream
ice

In a mixing glass with ice pour Kahlua and vodka. Stir and strain into a cocktail glass and float cream on top using a bar spoon.

Amazing Grapes

15 ml (1/2 fl oz) Metaxa brandy
15 ml (1/2 fl oz) Southern Comfort
30 ml (1 fl oz) apricot brandy
Sportsman Spumante
6 grapes
ice

In a highball glass with ice pour brandy, Southern Comfort and apricot brandy. Add 6 grapes and then top up with Sportsman Spumante.

Prize winning Australian recipe.

Pisco Sour

45 ml (1 1/2 fl oz) Inca Pisco
75 ml (2 1/2 fl oz) lime or lemon juice
8 ml (1/4 fl oz) Gomme syrup or 1 teaspoon
of sugar
2 dashes of Angostura bitters
dash of egg white
ice
maraschino cherry
slice of lemon

Shake all ingredients with ice except bitters. Strain into a sour glass then add bitters. Garnish with a cherry and slice of lemon.

Cuba Libre

8 ml (1/4 fl oz) lime juice
60 ml (2 fl oz) light rum
cola
ice
dash of Angostura bitters
1/2 slice of lime

Pour lime juice and light rum into a highball glass with ice and top up with cola, then put a dash of Angostura bitters on top. Garnish with lime.

Bazza Dazza

45 ml (1 1/2 fl oz) Jim Beam Bourbon
8 ml (1/4 fl oz) Cointreau
8 ml (1/4 fl oz) lime or lemon juice
cola

Pour into a highball glass with ice and top up with cola.

Punches

No 1 Booby Trap

ice
375 ml (13 fl oz) Drambuie
180 ml (6 fl oz) Rosso Antico
180 ml (6 fl oz) Bacardi rum (light)
375 ml (13 fl oz) Southern Comfort
champagne
375 ml (13 fl oz) orange juice
slice of lemon
slice of orange
strawberries (or tinned fruit salad
or any fruit in season)

In a punch bowl, with ice, add the Drambuie, Rosso Antico, Bacardi and Southern Comfort. Top up with champagne and orange juice. Garnish with slices of lemon and orange, and strawberries or other fruit.

Brandy Alexander Punch

Serves 12.

cracked ice
1 bottle 750 ml (26 fl oz) brandy
1/2 bottle 375 ml (13 fl oz) crème de cacao
1.5 litres (6 cups) fresh cream
nutmeg
maraschino cherries

Place cracked ice in punch bowl.
Mix all ingredients with an egg-beater till mixture starts to thicken.
Dust with nutmeg.
Add maraschino cherries (optional) and serve.

PUNCHES

In its oldest and simplest form Punch consisted of rum and water, hot or cold, with sugar to taste and orange or lemon juice (for Hot Punch) or fresh lime juice (for Cold Punch). During the eighteenth century this drink was very popular and was 'brewed' at the table in a punch bowl by the host with rum as one of the ingredients, but with other spirits as well.

AMERICAN PUNCH

ice cream
ice
180 ml (6 fl oz) bourbon
360 ml (12 fl oz) cherry brandy
180 ml (6 fl oz) blue curaçao
lemonade or 7-up

In a punch bowl add the ice cream. Pack ice at the sides of the punch bowl. Pour in the bourbon at the sides of the bowl. Carefully float the cherry brandy into the bowl, then the curaçao. Top up with lemonade or 7-up.

JUDY'S PUNCH

(Non-alcoholic)
To make approximately 20 drinks.

any fruit in season or substitute 2 450 g tins
fruit salad
cracked ice
375 ml (13 fl oz) lemon cordial
8 dashes Angostura bitters
1 large bottle (1 litre/32 fl oz) lemonade
1 large bottle (1 litre/32 fl oz) soda water
60 ml (2 fl oz) grenadine for colouring

Put the fruit in a punch bowl.
Mix the remaining ingredients and serve with fruit from the bowl.

KISSING THE BRIDE PUNCH

Serves 12

1 punnet strawberries
icing (confectioners') sugar
180 ml (6 fl oz) cognac
2 bottles (750 ml/26 fl oz) champagne

Place strawberries in a punch bowl and cover with sugar.
Add cognac and refrigerate for 6 to 8 hours.
Before serving, add champagne (well iced).
Note: It is not necessary to add ice to this punch.

PARTY PUNCH

To make approximately 25 drinks

1 bottle (750 ml/26 fl oz) Southern Comfort
120 ml (4 fl oz) Jamaican rum
120 ml (4 fl oz) lemon juice
240 ml (8 fl oz) pineapple juice
240 ml (8 fl oz) grapefruit juice
2 (750 ml/26 fl oz) bottles champagne
cracked or chipped ice
orange slices for garnish

Cool all ingredients then mix in a punch bowl.
Add champagne last and ice either cracked or chipped.
Garnish with orange slices and serve.

TEETOTALLER'S PUNCH

(Non-alcoholic)
To make approximately 20 drinks.

1/2 bottle (375 ml/13 fl oz) Clayton's Tonic
90 ml (3 fl oz) lemon juice
10 dashes Angostura bitters
2 (750 ml/26 fl oz) bottles dry ginger ale
1 (375 ml/13 fl oz) bottle lemonade
lemon slices

Mix all ingredients with cracked ice in a punch bowl, add lemon slices and serve.

KNOCKOUT PUNCH

To make approximately 25 drinks

1/2 bottle (375 ml/13 fl oz) Midori melon liqueur
180 ml (6 fl oz) crème de banane
1 bottle (750 ml/26 fl oz) vodka
600 ml (20 fl oz) cream
1 punnet strawberries (or fruit in season, or tinned fruit salad)
champagne or white sparkling wine

Mix all ingredients in a punch bowl, add cracked, chipped or block ice. Garnish with a punnet of strawberries. Lastly add champagne or white sparkling wine to taste.

PICK-ME-UPS

The 'morning after' misery is due to the effects of ethyl alcohol in your blood – your tongue is parched and feels as if you have licked the envelopes of all your Christmas mail in one night. You are cursing yourself for having that 'last one for the road' for now you have a first-rate hangover. But work must go on and you will not get sympathy from your boss nor your wife. Wherever you go you are told of sure-fire hangover cures but usually these are vile-tasting concoctions and don't work completely. But at least they give some consolation.

Upon rising, try deep breathing for this will send oxygen to your brain. And then try one of these simple remedies.

TOM AND JERRY

(Hot Punch)

eggs
caster (powdered) sugar
brandy
Jamaican rum
hot water
hot milk
nutmeg

Take as many eggs as there are persons to be served.
Beat the whites and yolks separately.
Add 1 teaspoon of sugar for each egg and mix whites with yolks.
When ready to serve, take 2 tablespoons of the egg mixture and pour into a large mug.
Add 30 ml (1 fl oz) brandy and 30 ml (1 fl oz) Jamaican rum (mixed together to avoid curdling). Fill to the top with hot water or hot milk, or half of each, and stir until smooth.
Sprinkle nutmeg on top and serve.
Note: This recipe can also be made with bourbon and brandy.

DANIELLE'S PUNCH

ice
cola
1.5 litres (40 fl oz) ice cream
whipped cream
cherries
thin slices oranges
hundreds and thousands
or grated chocolate

In a punch bowl, add ice and then pour cola until the bowl is one-quarter full. Add the ice cream and a layer of whipped cream. Garnish with cherries, orange slices; sprinkle with hundreds and thousands or grated chocolate.

FERNET BRANCA

This is à thick black bitters with quinine.

45 ml (1 1/2 fl oz) Fernet Branca
45 ml (1 1/2 fl oz) Pernod

Mix in old-fashioned glass with ice.

PRAIRIE OYSTER

Worcestershire sauce
2 drops Tabasco
yolk of fresh egg
salt and pepper to taste

In a champagne glass sprinkle Worcestershire sauce.
Add Tabasco and unbeaten egg yolk. Sprinkle with salt and pepper. Down in one gulp.

BUSH OYSTER

A Prairie Oyster with a beer chaser.

SKI LIFT

60 ml (2 fl oz) Fernet Branca or Underberg

Definition of a Ski Lift: after a big night out, the following morning the hands are shaky so try putting a towel around the back of your neck. Hold one end of the towel and the glass in the right hand and the other end of the towel in the left. Slowly elevate the right hand until the glass reaches the lips. If this cannot be accomplished then try Eddie's Cure – you are too sick to go anywhere.

EDDIE'S CURE

2 headache powders
1 glass water

Return to bed with this book.

NON-ALCOHOLIC DRINKS

NUT SPECIAL

3 cubes ice
any carbonated water
scoop ice cream
whipped cream
chopped nuts

In a tall glass put ice and half fill with your favourite carbonated water. Add a scoop of ice cream and then whipped cream with nuts sprinkled on top. Garnish with a strawberry and serve with a straw and parfait spoon.

LEMONADE

cracked ice
juice of 1 lemon
2 tablespoons sugar
water
slice of lemon

Fill a tall glass with cracked ice.
Add lemon juice and sugar.
Shake and pour unstrained into a glass.
Top with water.
Add a slice of lemon.
Serve with drinking straws.

MICKEY MOUSE

ice
cola
1 scoop ice cream
whipped cream
2 maraschino cherries

In a tall glass, with ice, pour cola.
Add 1 scoop of ice cream.
Top with whipped cream.
Serve with 2 cherries, a drinking straw and a spoon.

LIME, BITTERS AND SODA

ice
15 ml (¹/₂ fl oz) lime juice
soda water
3 drops Angostura bitters
slice of lemon

Fill a tall glass with ice. Add lime juice and top up with soda water. Add bitters and stir. Garnish with a slice of lemon.

EGG NOGG

1 egg
1 teaspoon caster (powdered) sugar
300 ml (10 fl oz) milk
ice
nutmeg or cinnamon
maraschino cherry

Shake egg, sugar and milk with ice.
Strain into a tall highball glass and dust with nutmeg or cinnamon.
Garnish with a cherry and serve with a drinking straw.

PUSSY CAT

1 cube sugar
dash Angostura bitters
tonic water
twist of lemon

In a champagne glass add sugar and bitters. Top up with tonic water and garnish with a twist of lemon.

Boo Boo's Special

8 ml (¹/₄ fl oz) lemon juice
90 ml (3 fl oz) pineapple juice
90 ml (3 fl oz) orange juice
dash Angostura bitters
dash grenadine
pineapple or fruit in season

In a cocktail shaker with
ice mix all the ingredients
together. Shake and serve
in a tall highball glass.
Top with water. Garnish
with fruit.

Kermit the Frog

2 cubes ice
lime soda
scoop ice cream
2 cherries

In a tall glass add ice and top up half way with lime
soda. Add ice cream. Garnish with cherries and
serve with a straw and a parfait spoon.

Claytons and Soda

45 ml (1¹/₂ fl oz) Claytons Tonic
soda water
ice
slice of lemon

Pour the Claytons into an old-fashioned glass with
ice. Top up with soda water and garnish with a
slice of lemon.

THE HISTORY OF BEER

The origin of brewing dates back to the time of the Pharoahs towards the end of the Fourth Dynasty. Ancient beer, known as Heqa (Rosetta Stone), came from Kati, a country to the east of Egypt.
By the year 2000 BC brewing was firmly established in Egypt. It was the daily drink for the Egyptians and was brewed from the waters of the Nile near the town of Thebes. Beer was believed to be a gift from the gods and the art of brewing was assigned to Isis, the wife of Osiris (Rameses II). Rameses promoted beer for consumption on all religious, social and state occasions.
The Greeks learned about brewing from the Egyptians and called it 'zythos' and even Sophocles recommended as the ideal diet – bread, meat, vegetables and beer. The Romans learned the art of brewing from the Greeks.

Even in India ancient Sanskrit law refers to alcoholic beverages prepared from barley, molasses and rice, so it is not surprising that literature of the Germanic races contained references to the manufacture of beer.

Brewing in England first appeared in Roman times but during the Anglo-Saxon period brewing became firmly established. It is believed that Edward the Confessor consumed ale at a banquet prior to the Battle of Hastings in 1066.

The monastic system flourished during the Middle Ages with each monastery having its own brewery with a monk in charge of brewing; each day he was allowed to consume two gallons of ale for tasting purposes.

Brewers often used many flavouring agents such as wormwood, alum, gentian and ground ivy and sometimes powdered oyster shells, aloes, bitter apples and bark of pine, oak and willow. The ground oyster shells were a clarifying agent, liquorice was used for colouring and was esteemed as gently laxative; it was also believed to prevent corpulence.

Even as late as the eighteenth century leading men of science believed that fermentation was caused by an electrical influence, and even until one hundred years ago, some people believed it to be supernatural.

In 1860 when Louis Pasteur proved fermentation was caused by micro-organisms he was ridiculed by all. But later Pasteur and others confirmed the connection between yeast and the transformation of sugars by fermentation.

In New South Wales the Pure Foods Act prescribes that beer shall be made from malt, sugar, hops and water, which contradicts the talk about beer being made from chemicals.

The amount of froth on the top of a glass of beer is a matter of individual preference, but a competent authority says: 'The head should be just above the rim of the glass, the collar extending about ½ inch (1.5 cm) from the top.' On the other hand, Victorians and Queenslanders do not like their beer to have much head, and if there is too much head it is common to hear: 'Why don't you put a tie on it as well?'

In Babylonian times if a glass of beer was served without a creamy head, the barmaid was drowned. Most people would agree this was severe but it shows how revered beer was.

Quality control is a major part of brewing and its aim is to ensure the consistency and uniformity of the product. Each brewery has a laboratory and its task is to test and measure throughout the brewing process. Because of this, beer has never been purer than it is at present.

Raw Materials used in Beer

Barley is preferred to other cereals as it can be more easily malted for brewing and the solubles extracted from barley malt are more complete than those of other grains.

When the grain has been steeped and dried, it is termed malt, and then it is ready for grinding or storing.

Hops belong to the nettle family. The female plants bear cone-shaped formations which are used in the brewing process. They impart a bitter flavour and pleasant aroma, increasing the refreshing quality, and stimulating digestion.

Actually any cereal containing starch or sugar may be used in the brewing of beer such as maize, rice, corn or wheat. But these grains are lacking in essential enzymes (chemicals which facilitate the extraction of sugars) and when used require special treatment. If used alone, the final product would not be beer as we know it in Australia.

Sugar is an important addition as it helps to produce a beer of paler colour, which is less filling, has a better taste and, of course, a greatly increased stability.

Brewers yeast is a micro-organism belonging to the *saccharomyces* species and is capable of a fantastic rate of reproduction. Its work is to propagate, which it does asexually, and splits up the sugar component into equal quantities of alcohol and carbon dioxide (CO_2). At this stage it may be well to mention that it is the CO_2 content of beer which determines the amount of foam formation. A consistent CO_2 level means that the bartender will not have any trouble handling beer at normal temperatures.

The brewing process

The barley is steeped until it germinates and is then kiln-dried to 90°C (180°F) to stop germination. It is then termed malt and is ready for grinding. The steps which follow involve mashing and fermentation.

Mashing

The crushed malt is mixed with water at a given temperature for the proper length of time. The resultant solution 'wort' is then used to make beer and the residue (spent grain) is sold as fodder for stock.

Fermentation

Fermentation is the next process where the yeast splits the sugars into alcohol and carbon dioxide. This is the most decisive phase in the brewing process for the attainment of brews of fine taste and aroma.

Composition of beer

The composition of a typical Australian beer is 91 percent water, 3.5 percent carbohydrates in the form of maltose and dextrins, 0.5 percent protein substance mineral salts, 0.42 percent carbon dioxide and 4 percent alcohol by weight. It also contains traces of essential vitamins, namely thiamine, niacin, riboflavin, pantothenic acid and pyridoxine.

What is lager beer?

Lager beer is distinguished by the fact that the wort is fermented by yeast of a bottom fermentation type (i.e. yeast which settles to the bottom of the fermenting tanks) and then is stored in refrigerated cellars for maturing and clarification. Lager got its name from the process the German brewers used to mature their *bier* in oak vats viz. 'lagering' which means 'to store'.

What is ale?

Traditionally, an ale is fermented by yeast of the top fermentation type and has a more pronounced hop flavour. Nowadays this term is often applied to some bottom fermentation beers with a pronounced hop flavour.

What is porter?

A top fermentation beer, porter is heavier and darker than ale, more malty in flavour, with less flavour of hops but sweeter in taste.

What is stout?

Top fermented stout is similar to porter. It has a strong flavour and a sweet taste, but is heavier and has a stronger hop character than porter.

What is pilsener?

Pilsener is a lager beer originally from the town of Pilsen in Germany. In the United States today there are approximately 150 breweries producing 350 brands of beer. Some of the better known brands are: Ballantine, Budweiser, Millers, Pabst, Schaefer and Schlitz.

Americans, who consume an average of about 17.2 gallons (77.4 litres) of beer per head a year, are obviously qualified beer lovers. And their beer should be served attractively in steins, pilsener glasses or foot o'ale glasses.

Old beer and new beer

Old beer is top fermentation English ale type and is the original type of beer brewed in Australia. It is the process that is old and has nothing to do with the maturation. New beer is a bottom fermentation lager type and is the more recent type of brewing process.

Old beer is not brewed in Western Australia, Victoria or Tasmania, and only very small quantities are brewed in South Australia and Queensland. Actually, new beer takes much longer to brew than old beer.

Glasses

The glasses used for beer-drinking should always be cool, clean and perfectly dry. When the beer is poured into a dry glass the air is trapped against the side and bottom of the glass and combines with the carbonic acid gas. A wet glass causes little air to be trapped and the result is flat beer.

The froth of various coloured liquids is always white. When liquids such as ales, champagnes and wines differ in colour, their froths, which are a collection of little spheres, are always white, due to the light which falls upon these and is reflected off the spheres.

Glasses for serving beer

These glasses need explaining as the names by which they are known vary from State to State.

A Middy in New South Wales is 300 ml (10 fl oz) but in Western Australia it is only 210 ml (7 fl oz). In other States it does not exist.

Popular beer drinks

In the United Kingdom, they prefer their beer at room temperature but in the United States and Australia it is preferred refrigerated. There are many variations of beer recipes. Some Europeans will drink a shot of Schnapps with a beer chaser. Americans are known to have a shot of whisky with a beer chaser which is called a 'Boilermaker'. A 'Red Eye' is beer and tomato juice.

In the United Kingdom and Australia a shandy is beer and lemonade. In the United States a shandy gaff is half beer and half ginger beer. Further variations half and half American – half fill a glass with beer and top up with porter; an 'Arf and 'Arf English – half fill a glass with beer and top up with ale.

GLOSSARY

ADVOKAAT — A Dutch liqueur made from egg yolks, sugar and brandy.

AERATED WATER — Mineral water.

ALMOND SYRUP — Syrup made of sweet almonds and water.

AMARETTO — Almond flavoured liqueur.

AMARETTO DI GALLIANO — An almond flavoured liqueur from Italy

AMER PICON — A French aperitif wine.

AMOURETTE — A violet-coloured French liqueur.

AMSTERDAM — A liqueur containing Cherry Brandy and Advokaat.

ANGELICA — A very sweet Basque liqueur flavoured with angelica.

ANISETTE — A very sweet colourless aniseed-flavoured liqueur.

APERITIF — Low alcoholic content drink taken before meals and designed to sharpen the appetite.

APPLE BRANDY OR APPLEJACK — Brandy distilled from apple wine.

APPLE CIDER — Fermented apple juice.

APRICOT BRANDY — A highly-flavoured liqueur made from apricots.

AQUAVIT — Scandinavian liqueur made from potatoes and flavoured with caraway seeds.

ARMAGNAC — A French grape brandy.

ARRACK — Any Eastern spirituous liquor, especially one made from coco palm. Different countries use various ingredients but rice is also commonly used in this liquor.

AURUM — A pale gold Italian liqueur of orange flavour – not too sweet.

BAILEYS IRISH CREAM — Made from the finest old whiskey and Irish cream.

BENEDICTINE D.O.M. — A sweet, herb-flavoured, brandy-based liqueur. One of the oldest liqueurs in the world and originally made by Benedictine monks. Can be mixed with equal parts of brandy and known as B. & B. Benedictine is sometimes referred to as D.O.M. liqueur (Deo optimo maximo) of the Benedictine Order.

BITTERS — Sometimes referred to as aromatic bitters, this infusion of aromatics contains roots and herbs and is used sparingly to flavour. Bitters are made in a similar way to liqueurs, without sweetening and are designed to aid the appetite. Best known bitters are Angostura (Trinidad), Amer Picon (France), Campari (Italy) and Cinzano (Italy).

BLACKBERRY BRANDY — A very dark liqueur flavoured with blackberries.

BLACKCURRANT LIQUEUR — Liqueur made from blackcurrants, brandy and sugar; also known under its French name Cassis.

BOILERMAKER — A shot of straight Scotch followed by beer chaser.

BRANDY — Distilled from fermented juices of ripe grapes and other fruits. When sweetening is added it then is usually referred to as a liqueur.

BRONTE — A brandy based liqueur with honey taste.

BYRRH — A French aperitif.

CALVADOS — Apple brandy from Normandy.

CAMPARI — An Italian aperitif wine with strong bitter taste.

CAMPARI WHITE — A sweet liqueur made from maceration of fresh raspberries and aged in oak casks. Served after dinner, very cold.

CHAMBERY — A very dry vermouth from the district of Chambery, France.

CHARTREUSE — A liqueur made from many different roots, spices and herbs. There are two types: yellow which is light, and green which is heavy and stronger in spirit strength.

CHERI-SUISE — A chocolate cherry liqueur.

CHERRY BRANDY — A liqueur containing juice of ripe cherries.

CHIANTI — Dry Italian wine mostly red in colour but white is available.

CHOCOLATE PEPPERMINT — Made from a balance of chocolate and mint.

CLAYTON'S TONIC — Non-alcoholic kola.

CLEOPATRA — A brown liqueur with chocolate and orange flavour.

COFFEE BRAZIL — Made from Brazilian coffee and jamaican rum.

COINTREAU — A sweet, colourless liqueur with orange flavour.

CORDIAL-MEDOC	A dark red French liqueur.
CREME D'ANANAS	A pineapple liqueur with a rum base.
CREME DE BANANE	A brandy-based liqueur with banana flavour.
CREME DE CASSIS	A liqueur with blackcurrant flavour.
CREME DE CACAO	A very sweet dark brown liqueur made from cocoa beans, vanilla and spices and has cocoa flavour.
CREME DE FRAISES	A sweet French liqueur, strawberry in colour and flavoured with strawberries.
CREME DE FRAMBOISES	A sweet French liqueur, raspberry in colour and flavoured with raspberries.
CREME DE MARRONS GLACÉS	An Italian liqueur with a full bodied natural flavour and the fragrance and creamy mellowness of melted marrons glacé.
CREME DE MENTHE	A peppermint-flavoured liqueur which comes in three colours – green, white or red.
CREME DE MOKA	A light brown French liqueur with coffee flavour.
CREME DE NOISETTES	Sweet liqueur made from edible nuts.
CREME DE NOYEAUX	Almond flavoured French liqueur made from apricot and peach pits. Comes in pink and white.
CREME DE ROSES	A pink liqueur, flavoured with roses.
CREME DE VANILLE	A sweet French liqueur with strong vanilla flavour.
CREME DE VIOLETTES	A pale violet French liqueur with violet scent.
CREME YVETTE	A sweet American liqueur with the flavour, colour and scent of Parma violets.
CURAÇAO	A sweet digestive liqueur made with wine or grape spirit, sugar and peel from oranges grown on island of Curaçao – orange, blue, green and white colours.
DAMSON GIN	An English liqueur flavoured with damson and dark red in colour.
DANZIGER	A liqueur with gold leaf floating through it.
DRAMBUIE	A liqueur based on Scotch Whisky and heather honey.
DUBONNET	A dark red French aperitif wine with red wine base and a slight quinine taste.
ELIXIR D'ANVERS	A sweet yellow liqueur, similar taste to Yellow Chartreuse.
FERNET BRANCA	Italian bitters.
FIOR D'ALPE	A liqueur flavoured with flowers and herbs grown on slopes of the Alps. Extremely sweet – sugar forms crystals in bottle.
FORBIDDEN FRUIT	A red flame-coloured American liqueur. The flavour is mixture of grapefruit and orange, it is sweet with a bitter after-taste.
FRAISE DES BOIS	A fresh strawberry liqueur which has been a secret recipe of the Dolfi family for three generations. The smallest strawberries of the Alsace region are pressed into a juice with fine alcohol and a pure sugar syrup.
FRAISIA	A French liqueur red in colour with strawberry flavour.
GALLIANO	A gold-coloured liqueur with licorice and anisette flavour.
GAMADA	Coffee liqueur made from coffee from the Papua New Guinea Highlands.
GLAYVA	A liqueur from Scotland, similar to Drambuie.
GLEN MIST	A liqueur similar to Drambuie, but containing mixture of Irish and Scottish whiskies.
GOCCIA D'ORO	Made from oranges from Messina, together with orange blossom fragrance and blended with citrus oils.
GOMME SYRUP	Sugar syrup – made by heating 500 g (1 lb) sugar in 2½ cups (20 fl oz) of water, slowly stirring until it comes to the boil (do not let it boil).
GRAND MARNIER	A golden-brown French brandy liqueur, with orange flavour.
GRAPPA	Italian spirit made from the skins, pips and stalks of grapes after wine is made.
GRANDE LIQUEUR	A French liqueur made in two colours, yellow and green, with chartreuse flavour.
GRENADINE	Red artificial flavouring used for sweetness.
GREEN GINGER WINE	Wine made from fruit and Jamaican ginger.

ACKNOWLEDGEMENTS

The Publishers would like to thank the following companies for providing props.
Statements, Paddington
Kosta Boda, Artarmon
The Glass House, Brookvale
KWL Imports Pty Ltd, Sydney
Incorporated Agencies, Redfern
Orrefors, Chatswood
Finnish Importing, Northbridge
Village Living, Avalon
Ron Hyndman, Ultimo
Breville

Managing Editor: Susan Tomnay
Editor: Diane Furness
Design: Willy Richards

Published by Lansdowne Press, Sydney
a division of RPLA Pty Limited
176 South Creek Road, Dee Why West, N.S.W., Australia, 2099.
First published 1983
Reprinted 1985
© Copyright RPLA Pty Limited 1983.
Produced in Australia by the Publisher
Typeset in Australia by Walter Deblaere & Associates

Printed in Hong Kong
by South China Printing Co.
National Library of Australia
Cataloguing-in-Publication Data
Tirado Eddie.
  Cocktails and mixed drinks.
  2nd ed. Previous ed.: Sydney: Lansdowne Press, 1982.
  Includes index.

ISBN 0 7018 1784 4.
1. Cocktails.   2.Alcoholic beverages.
I. Title.
641.8'74